CULTIVATING FIRE

How to Keep Your Motivation White Hot

Adam Khan

ISBN-10: 0962465666
ISBN-13: 978-0962465666

Published in the USA

YouMe Works Publishing

DEDICATION

A lot of things need to be done in this world — problems to solve, challenges to overcome, and discoveries and inventions and creations yet to be brought forth. This book is dedicated to what is wanted and needed in this world. May the fire you cultivate be used for good.

CONTENTS

ACKNOWLEDGMENTS

I'd like to thank my wife, Klassy Evans, for her endless encouragement of my writing. I literally wouldn't be doing this without her guidance and inspiration. And I would like to express my appreciation to the motivational writers who lit me on fire early in life, especially Napoleon Hill, Earl Nightingale, W. Clement Stone, and Brian Tracy. And I'd like to say "Thanks Mom" for showing me all those years ago what motivation can do.

Introduction

"Man is by nature a productive organism. When he ceases his productivity — whether he is producing a pail or a poem, an industry or an ideology — his life begins to lose its meaning. Though he may be finally buried twenty years after his death, the person who has no *raison d'être* is not really alive. He is merely the ghost of who he once was or might have become."

- Allen Wiesen

IF YOU want to feel better and get more done, your first requirement is at least one goal. You need something to aim at. Human beings are goal-achieving at their best. This is one of the most basic principles of success, happiness, sanity, and mental health.

Once you have something to aim for, you have two things to concern yourself with: Motivation and demoralization. I've written about demoralization in the book, *Antivirus For Your Mind.* You can use it to prevent setbacks from *taking away* your motivation. But can anything be done to increase or even *maintain* your motivation? And is there anything else besides setbacks that can take away your motivation? Yes indeed.

When you first create a goal, you are already motivated. The moment you choose it, you're motivated. You chose the goal in the first place *because* you're motivated to accomplish it.

But what happens? Your motivation tends to fade, doesn't it?

Why?

One very significant reason motivation fades is that *you think of new goals*, and they seem better somehow. You haven't gotten bogged down in the details of the *new* goal yet. Your new goal seems clean and pristine and more appealing than the goal you are slogging toward at the moment, full of problems and difficulties (or, if you prefer, *challenges* and *opportunities*).

Interruptions and distractions are also major forces that can dampen that once-hot-burning fire of desire.

But a more practical way of thinking about the causes of demotivation is that it happens simply because you haven't done much to keep yourself motivated.

Motivation will *naturally* fade. Some people are disheartened by this fact. But it is not a problem. *Motivation doesn't last.* Okay. But it can be reborn. It can be renewed, and it *needs* to be renewed and refreshed regularly. Just like a fire, motivation can be regularly stoked.

When you bathe, your state of cleanliness does not last forever either. You have to bathe again and again if you want to stay clean. But so what?

And when you exercise, it does not make you permanently fit. You'll have to exercise again and again to get and stay fit. So what? That is what it takes, so that's you do.

You may never have put motivation in the same category, but now that you think about it, I'm sure you can see that it *must* be in the same category. There is no reason to believe that either you're motivated or you're not and there is nothing you can do about it. Just like your fitness level and your state of cleanliness, there is *plenty* you can do about it.

The question is, of course, "*How* can motivation be refreshed?" *How* can you enhance your own motivation? How can you boost it when it's sagging? How can you keep it strong?

MOTIVATION IS IMPORTANT

A feeling of motivation isn't just nice, it is powerful and important. The difference between someone motivated and someone unmotivated is like the difference between a race car and a moped. A motivated person can accomplish far more and is far more capable than an unmotivated person.

I once worked as a waiter in a new restaurant and the bussers were all high school students from the local area — an upscale, wealthy area. These kids didn't need the money. In fact, some of them only worked because their parents thought it would be "good for them" to have a job.

These kids were not very motivated. They had the potential to do a good job, but without motivation, they didn't even come *close* to fulfilling that potential.

The waiters tipped the bussers. That's how the bussers made *most* of their money. The waiters, of course, tried to motivate them by letting them know we'd tip more if they worked harder, but most of them didn't really care. They were more interested in just going through the motions of their job, and talking to the opposite sex.

Then the restaurant began to hire immigrants from Mexico for the busser positions. The contrast was astonishing. These Mexicans did about three times the work of the high school students. Why?

They weren't physically healthier or any smarter than the high school students. They were definitely *not* more well-rested — most of the Mexicans were working two jobs.

But they were *motivated.*

When they worked hard, we tipped them more. And the money we gave them was worth a lot more back in Mexico than it was in the U.S.

Many of them had a wife and kids, and were often supporting their parents and sisters as well, and many were saving up their money to start a business or buy a house back in Mexico.

They were very *motivated* and the contrast between them and the well-fed, young, well-rested high school students was sharp and dramatic.

Motivation makes a *huge* difference. It's hard to overstate. Imagine what a difference it could make to you and your goals.

Whether or not you achieve *your* goals depends *almost entirely* on your motivation. Think about that. Let it sink in.

It's possible that you will never achieve your goals. But if you do, it will be because you were motivated and *stayed* motivated. If you *don't* achieve your goals, it will be because you weren't motivated enough. This simple, fundamental truth is easy to overlook.

And it doesn't really matter if you are motivated right *now*. Motivation changes constantly, like all feelings.

But your feelings of motivation can be cultivated and can grow more *intense*, or your feelings of motivation can be neglected and fade away. It is largely up to you.

If maintaining your motivation seems like work — if it seems tedious or odious, you're thinking of it all wrong. Motivation is *fun*. Feeling motivated is a great feeling. It makes you want to get out of bed in the morning and hit the ground running because you have things you *can't wait* to do. Motivation makes you feel *alive*.

And tremendous things are possible to someone who is motivated and can *stay* motivated.

There are people all over the world who accomplish extraordinary things, and many of them are merely ordinary people with ordinary talents — but with extraordinary motivation. And it was not something they were born with.

Listen to me very carefully. This is important. They weren't *born* with motivation. The reason they now have extraordinary motivation is that they're doing certain things that cultivate their motivation. And they do specific things that prevent their motivation from withering.

Cultivate is the key word. You don't cultivate an apple tree once and for all. Cultivation is an *ongoing* task. If you pull weeds and add water and fertilizer and prune it, the tree can grow robust and healthy.

Let it fend for itself, however, and it will probably become weak. It'll be choked by weeds. It will dry out. It might be infested with pests, so the leaves will have holes in them, the branches might grow too close together or sprawl so they'll produce fewer and smaller apples. The tree might even wither and die.

Here you are now, with a goal and motivated to whatever degree. Let's see what we can do to cultivate your motivation — to make it healthy and robust, vital and intense.

The question is: What is motivation's "water and fertilizer?" The chapters that follow answer this question.

I once heard a phrase that has stuck with me. When you make a list or chart your progress or put a motivational slogan on your bathroom mirror, you are creating "a structure of fulfillment." You're making your *progress* easier. You're making it easier for your goals to be accomplished. You're making the fulfillment of your desires more likely.

Think of it like a trellis. Many bean plants are vines, and if you just let them grow naturally, they will grow along the ground, making them more vulnerable to pests and rot, and they won't get as much sun if there are other plants around.

But give them a trellis to climb on, and they can *thrive*. They will be healthier and produce more beans. They can come closer to fulfilling their true potential.

The trellis is a structure that makes it possible for the plant to fulfill its potential yield. It can't yield as much without that structure, even though its genetics haven't changed, the soil, the sun, the weather haven't changed. It won't do as well without that structure to climb on.

The same is true of you. If you make structures to help you, you can fulfill more of your potential. So let's be clear about this: An important factor in cultivating a feeling of motivation is creating *structures of fulfillment* that make success easier or faster, because *success is motivating*.

The principles in the following chapters are structures of fulfillment. They will help you maintain a strong level of motivation.

And your high motivation can make it possible for you to accomplish your most heartfelt goals.

Let us begin.

Prune Your Goals

THE MORE goals you have, the less likely any one of them will be achieved. The more goals you have, the slower your progress on any one of them. And *slow progress is demotivating*. Anything you do that slows down your accomplishment or makes your goal seem *less* possible will suck out your motivation like a lamprey.

Prune your goals so you have fewer goals, and you automatically preserve your motivation better.

There is only one problem with this: Complexity will keep creeping in. The natural drift of your life and mind is *toward complexity*.

You have only twenty-four hours in a day. Time is limited, and if you want to stay motivated, your goals need to be limited too. Not limited in the sense of setting only small goals, but limited to a small enough *number* of goals that they don't bog you down with complexity. Keep them trimmed and your motivation can stay high. Keep them trimmed and progress can be rapid and enlivening.

Stephen Hawking, the physicist and mathematician, has Amyotrophic Lateral Sclerosis, a disease that handicaps his movement and speech. Hawking wouldn't wish his disease on anyone, but in many ways it is the secret of his success. His condition has forced him to limit the scope of his activities. Many common distractions and diversions were unavailable to him, so he concentrated on what *was* available (using his mind) and became a world-renowned thinker and theoretician — the top thinker in his field. His condition *forced* him to keep his goals pruned, allowing him to focus.

I'm referring to this as "pruning" goals rather than "dropping some goals" because the process has to be *continual.*

Just as tree branches keep growing, your list of goals will keep growing. You don't prune once and for all — you can't. You have to *keep* doing it.

If you have an apple tree and you take care of it, you'll prune it every year and the tree will become healthier, it'll produce more apples, and the apples will be bigger. That's the purpose of pruning, and the same goes for you and your goals.

Your goals can reach greater fruition, and can happen faster, if you keep your goals pruned to just a few, or even one.

You may only have one main goal right now. You may not have any goals to prune *at the moment.* But give it some time. Goals tend to increase and accumulate, weighing you down and slowing progress, until you are overwhelmed with too much to do and too few results showing from all your effort. This is discouraging.

Discouragement hampers motivation.

The way to prevent it or cure it is to sit down and list your goals, and then try your best to prune some of them. Either give them up, or put them in a file to be accomplished some other time, basically giving them up for now and maybe forever.

This is hard to do. And it's hard for the same reason it's hard to throw away something you own, even if you haven't used it in years. After all, you may still want to use it in the future, right? In effect, the object you don't want to throw away represents a goal. It might be an old tennis racket you haven't used, but it represents a goal to play tennis "some day."

There is a certain degree of built-in greed we all have. We want to *own,* we want to *accumulate.* Not just *physical possessions* but also future accomplishments. That's why giving up a goal is difficult.

But it has to be done. You have to throw away (or at least set aside) perfectly good and desirable goals. You have to curb your natural greed by practicing the virtue of simplicity. Learn to appreciate simplicity and focus, and appreciate them so much you're willing to suffer the pruning.

The more goals you have, the more distracted you are. And I'm not just talking about only your *stated* goals. Someone might spend three hours a day watching television and yet not think of it as a "goal." They might spend more actual uninterrupted time watching television than they spend on any other activity, and not ever consider it one of their goals. But it is *functioning* as a goal. And a very important one, given how much time they spend on it. Relaxation or entertainment or escape must be an important goal of theirs. If not, they should do something about it.

If you ever notice that the amount of time you spend on something doesn't match how important you feel it is, it's time to prune that goal. You don't have to go overboard. Everyone needs a certain amount of downtime or rest. But you can *prune* your goals until they reflect your true values.

You can spend a week logging everything you do all day, and how long you do it. Then add up the hours for each kind of activity. If it reflects the things you really care about, you know you're on track. If it doesn't, decide what to spend less time on, and what you want to drop completely.

Make sure the way you spend your time is congruent with what you really care about. Your congruency can significantly increase your motivation.

But here's the bottom line: To stay motivated you need to be very selective about what goals you choose to pursue. And you need to *regularly* prune the extra goals you will tend to accumulate.

Keep your goals narrowed down to only a few or even just one, and you will be able to focus, and *focus* is one of the most important factors of motivation.

The more goals you have, the less focused you can be.

The fewer your goals, the *more* focused you can be. And the more focused you are, the faster your progress, and *fast progress is motivating.*

Make a List, Put it in Order

IMAGINE you are facing an enormous pile of chopped wood that must be stacked neatly against a wall. The pile is so huge, your stacking job will take weeks to finish. The moment you are told you must do this, you feel like you'd been kicked in the stomach. Sometimes the sheer *size* of a big project can demoralize you.

But let's say I was your boss and asked you to just pick up one particular log and stack it against the wall. How does that feel? Easy, right? When you come back, I ask you, "pick up this one here and stack it next to the other one." Piece of cake. My requests are simple and easy. They're not overwhelming at all.

That's what making a list and putting it in order will do for you: It prevents a big project from overwhelming you. It is *demotivating* to have a large, unorganized mess to sort out. But doing one thing after another toward a goal you really want, seeing regular progress, and crossing off the items as you complete them, is very motivating.

Once you set your goal, you're in the same position as having one big pile of wood to stack. It is a mess. It's confusing and enormous. You may not even know where to start. You may feel overwhelmed. I know people who don't get any further with important goals than just thinking of a goal that would truly satisfy them (and that they could actually accomplish if they put in the work), but then they feel overwhelmed because it's such a big goal (and they underestimate their own capability), and then they abandon the idea right there.

In other words, they think of the big pile of wood, feel completely dwarfed and belittled by the idea, and give up on the spot. The goal hardly had time to be imagined before it died.

It doesn't have to be like that. There is one good way to tackle a big goal: Make a list and put it in order.

Make a list of what you need to do, and put it in the order it needs to be done. This is one of the most powerful principles of accomplishment ever invented.

Alan Lakein is the author of the most famous book on time management ever written: *How to Get Control of Your Time and Your Life*. When Lakein first started out, he simply asked successful people how they accomplished so much. The first person he interviewed said, "I make a to-do list."

Lakein went on with the interview, almost dismissing that answer as too commonplace.

But the next high-powered executive he interviewed gave an almost identical answer. And the next. And the next. The principle — make a list — is so simple, so basic, so commonplace, and so totally unremarkable, it doesn't seem to be worth doing. But it works, and it works better than anything else.

But there is one thing you have to do to make it work: You actually have to make a list and put it in order.

This method doesn't *necessarily* make you motivated. But it can prevent you from becoming demotivated by the hugeness and complexity of your goal.

You're already motivated. You chose your goal because you're motivated to achieve it. But once you start working on it, you can feel discouraged when you fully grasp the size or complexity of the thing you decided to do.

Imagine you're a gladiator and you step into an arena expecting to face someone your own size, knowing you have skill and strength and feeling fairly confident...but what you see is a hundred men walking into the arena. Realistically, you have no chance of winning. You might not be motivated to even try.

Setting a large goal for yourself can be overwhelming in the same way, and can take away your motivation just as fast.

But what if you (as a gladiator) could fight the hundred men *one at a time*, a different one every day? You'd have a chance. And *because* you had a chance, you wouldn't lose your fighting spirit so easily.

That is what a list does for you. It takes this large group of tasks, this big mess, this big army, and makes them line up in single file so you can deal with them one at a time. This makes your goal feel more possible. And it actually makes you — in reality — more likely to achieve that goal.

When a goal feels more possible, it not only prevents demotivation, it keeps you focused. I spent most of yesterday, for example, cleaning up loose ends, doing email, searching for a song I'd heard and wanted to buy, and finding a book (online), etc. — in other words, I piddled away my time until it ran out and I had to go to bed.

I didn't make a to-do list yesterday. Sometimes I don't. If I had made a list yesterday, none of the things I just mentioned would have been on it. And if I was working from a list, I would have either not done those things, or hurried through them in half the time (because they aren't important to completing my list, and since my list is a consciously-chosen list of what is important to me, they weren't really important, period).

That kind of frittering away time is not at all unusual. It is sobering how much time almost all of us waste on unimportant things when we haven't made a list.

One way to stay motivated, then, is to break a large task into its smallest units and do those one at a time. You are essentially breaking your larger goal down into smaller targets — reachable, achievable targets. Aiming for that kind of target makes you want to get up off your duff and get at it.

The way I wrote this series of books (*Antivirus For Your Mind*, *Slotralogy*, *Viewfinder*, and this one) is a good example. I'd accumulated material for years, and the file was enormous. I didn't know where to start.

So I read through the file, just reading each piece of paper, and started a list of principles or methods. When I was done, I had about twenty principles, but I realized some were really subcategories of others, so I wrote out a shorter list with subcategories. I got it down into a smaller number of principles.

All the material in my file fit into one of those categories, so I sat down on the floor and sorted all the material into piles, one for each category.

It already felt less overwhelming. I was beginning to have something I could work with. Then I put those principles (one principle per pile) in order. Then I took the first principle (with its own stack of notes) and set the others aside. Now this single principle was my project — which was much smaller and less overwhelming.

I sorted the items in *that* pile into order (some were best mentioned before others), gave it some thought, and finally I could begin writing.

In other words, I took a big, intimidating project, broke it up and sorted it, and then it wasn't intimidating in the slightest.

Whatever your goal, when you sit down to make a list, simply break your goal into pieces — projects or tasks. Basically you're breaking your big goal into smaller subgoals. If those pieces aren't small enough, put them in the order they should be done and then take the first one and break *that* one into pieces.

Then put *those* in order. Some tasks need to be done before the other ones. Some tasks are more important than the others. Put them in the best order you can.

Now take the first one. You *only* have to think of that one now. You do not need to think about the others — you've got them written down so you won't forget them. You can take your attention off of them for now. Concentrate on the first item until it's finished. Then cross it off, take a moment to enjoy that, and then look at the next one. And so on.

This way of working keeps you focused. Focus helps keep you motivated. Sidetracks have a harder time worming their way into your activity, slowing down your progress and diluting your motivation.

Another nice feature of working this way — besides the motivation and lack of demoralization — is the satisfaction you get. Often modern tasks leave no visible impression. They may be necessary and important, but when the day is done, it doesn't *feel* as if you've really gotten *anything* accomplished.

For example, I've been working all night editing this book. When I'm done, I will shut down my computer. There will be no visible indication I've done a darned thing today, but I spent nine hours working! That kind of thing can feel demotivating. Your actions seem futile. Or at least it can be a lot *more* motivating and invigorating to have some visible indication you're moving toward your goal.

When you make a list and check off the tasks as you do them, by the end of the day you have a record, a *visible* record, of your accomplishments. It makes you feel more satisfied and helps keep you motivated.

The principle is simple but *very powerful*: Make a list and put it in order. It is an important key to keeping your motivation strong.

Keep the Challenge Just Right

ONE VERY common motivation-killer is trying to deal with too much at one time and feeling overwhelmed. The two solutions to that, as we've just covered are:

1. Prune your goals
2. Make a list, and put it in order

Those two work because they help keep your challenge level just right. If the challenge is too great, it produces stress and demoralization — in other words, it is demotivating. If the challenge is too small, however, it makes you feel bored, and that is also demotivating.

To keep your motivation high, to keep your interest, to keep your concentration engaged, you've got to keep your level of challenge in that middle place where your skill matches the skill required, or at least comes close. That is difficult sometimes. But you're getting the tools here to make it possible.

The first step is to understand what makes a goal challenging.

Whether or not something is a challenge is determined by how much skill it requires to do successfully. If something is very challenging, it requires a lot of skill or capability. If it is not very challenging, it requires very little skill or capability.

For example, in an experiment at Virginia Polytechnic Institute and State University, every day for four days, two groups of women did as many sit ups as they could in 90 seconds. This was a *challenge*. This was a *test* of their *physical capability*. But the purpose of the experiment was to test two different ways to deal with a challenge, and it gives us an insight into how to keep the level of the challenge just right.

The first group was merely told to do their very best — to do as many sit ups as they could.

The researchers gave the second group specific targets, such as "do ten percent more than you did last time."

Which group do you think did more sit ups? The first group averaged 43 sit ups, and the number didn't change over the four days. The second group averaged 56 sit ups by the last day. They had become more capable as the experiment went on.

Why? Because they managed their challenge. "Doing your best" is almost impossible. It's too vague. If you're doing sit ups and your muscles are hurting, can you do one more sit up? Probably, but you might hurt yourself. So where do you stop? If your life depended on it, you could probably do even one more. It's a challenge that is too open-ended. There is really no way to "succeed" at the task, and that isn't very motivating.

On the other hand, doing "ten percent more" puts the challenge within reach. It is still challenging, but it is such a small improvement, it seems within reach, so it isn't an overwhelming challenge. And they could succeed. They could accomplish the goal of ten percent more. A target that seems challenging but within reach is motivating. The challenge level is kept just right.

Last week I had been editing my web site all day, so I took a break. It was early evening, and I was going to sit down and edit some more, but I'd had enough. My brain felt drained. I was fairly close to finishing one page, however, so I thought, "I could just finish that page and then call it a day."

Instantly I had plenty of motivation. Why? Because I put the challenge within reach. It wasn't "all or nothing." Working for some unknown length of time made me tired just to think of it, kind of like the instruction to "do your best." But the possibility of working for a *limited* time to finish a specific page was motivating, and I was able to squeeze a little more from myself.

You can manage your challenge in many different ways, and it will have a good influence on your motivation level. You'll get more done and you'll get it done faster, and the whole thing will feel better.

The main principle here is to keep the challenge just right by aiming for goals that are difficult but within reach if you really try.

Difficult but attainable goals keep you at the upper edge of your skill level, and when you're in that zone, your concentration and motivation is at its highest. You get a lot done and you feel good doing it.

Videogame programmers have mastered the technique of always keeping the player at the upper edge of his skill. The game carefully manages your challenge for you. As soon as you master one level, you get to go to a slightly more challenging level. People spend hours at a time totally focused, totally motivated, and they do it *voluntarily* — they do it for fun. It is so motivating, some people often feel they shouldn't be doing it, but they do it anyway because the feeling of being in that zone at a perfect level of challenge is very pleasurable. It is almost addicting, it feels so good.

If you manage the challenges of your goal with equal care, your goal can become very pleasurable, and even addicting. If you manage the challenge so it stays in that place between stressful and boring — if you can keep yourself at the upper edge of your skill — your goal can become totally engrossing and intensely attractive. And of course, as you do that, your skill level increases, so you'll need to keep adjusting your challenge upward to stay in the zone.

MORE THAN TIME SPENT

Scientists have tried to figure out why some people who spend a lot of time doing something, like golfing for example, get very good at it, while others, who also spend a lot of time, never get much better. What they have discovered is that it isn't only time that counts, but what they called "effortful study."

Effortful study means a person tries to push herself to the upper reaches of her skill (playing against people slightly better than she is, for example) and when she beats them, finding someone a little better, etc., all the while concentrating on improving; on studying if necessary, on watching films of her strokes, etc.

This is in sharp contrast to someone who really loves to golf and plays every weekend with a buddy who has about equal skill. Sometimes one wins, and sometimes the other wins. Neither have much motivation to get tremendously *better* because then they'd beat their friend all the time, and what fun would that be?

The two are motivated, but they are motivated to hang out together rather than motivated to play their way into the big leagues. They might both get slightly better over time, and they might not. But their enjoyment will come mostly from their *relationship*, not from the accomplishment of some goal. The challenge is fairly low because they're not aiming at something difficult.

That is different than the challenge set by a high goal. Your feeling of motivation will depend to some degree on whether you're aiming too high or too low or just right. If you have set your sights on the upper edge of what you believe is within your reach, the goal will feel challenging, but not impossible.

If you feel your goal is impossible (aiming too high), or if you suspect it *might* be impossible, that will kill your motivation. You might even set a goal *that is actually possible for you*, but if you don't *believe* it is possible, you'll feel your goal is hopeless. You will feel helpless to achieve it, so your motivation will be weak, even if you really *could* achieve it if you tried.

THE BENCHMARK

Bear with me now. I'm going to get a little technical for a few pages, but it will clarify something important we'll use later. Julian Simon, the author of *Good Mood*, developed a model of how to manage the level of challenge. It's a good way to think about what's going on. Simon says the *actual state* compared with the *benchmark state* is what determines your happiness.

In other words, what determines whether you feel good or not is how you compare where you are with where you want to be. It's how you compare the *actual* state to the *benchmark* state. Let me explain what this means.

The *actual state* is your real circumstances and your feelings. The *benchmark state* is what you want your circumstances to be, and how you want to feel. In other words, the benchmark state is how you think you *should* feel, where you think you *ought* to be at this stage of your life, where you wanted to be by the time you were your age, etc. It's a benchmark. It's a goal you have decided to reach. It's a state you want to be in.

Julian Simon's concepts cast a revealing light on our task of keeping the level of challenge just right.

David Burns, author of *Feeling Good*, works on the actual state. His emphasis is on what he calls "distorted thinking," that is, *misperceiving* the actual state. His method is to dig up and root out mistakes in thinking. Cognitive distortions (thought-mistakes) are a misperception of the actual state. So if you are actually capable, but you think you *aren't*, you're misperceiving the actual state.

A pioneer in the cognitive therapy field, Albert Ellis, works on modifying your *benchmark* state so it's more realistic.

According to Ellis, nothing is wrong with goals and expectations. Where we go wrong is demanding that the actual state matches the benchmark by thinking in terms of should, ought, and must — commanding and demanding that the world live up to our desires and expectations.

It is unrealistic to insist that reality should and must match your ideals. For example, is it realistic to expect *all* people to like you all the time? No. A benchmark like that would create unnecessary suffering. Every time someone didn't like you would make you feel bad.

As another example: Is it realistic to expect your challenging goal to be *easy* to accomplish? No.

A benchmark like that would make you feel demoralized by even a minor setback.

Martin Seligman, author of *Learned Optimism*, deals with your sense of hopelessness or helplessness about achieving the benchmark. If you feel demoralized, you have one of three options (besides simply getting depressed):

1. Change your *benchmark* (lower it to something you truly believe you could achieve).

2. Correct your misperception of your *ability* so you recognize you are not helpless about achieving your goal.

3. Correct your misperception of reality so your *recognize* that the accomplishment of your goal isn't hopeless.

You can see that #2 and #3 are the same as David Burns' work. Your sense of hopelessness is a subcategory of the actual state. In other words, you can correct your misperception by asking yourself, "Am I *actually* helpless? Is it *really* hopeless? Or have I misperceived the real situation? Do I perhaps have more ability than I've given myself credit for? Are the barriers really as huge and insurmountable as I believe they are?"

David Burns, Martin Seligman, Albert Ellis, and Julian Simon are all working in the field of cognitive therapy. That is, they are helping people overcome anxiety and depression by helping them change the way they habitually think.

The way you think can prevent you from keeping the level of challenge just right for you.

MOTIVATIONAL MATERIAL

Another category of cognitive "therapy" is the whole genre of motivational seminars, success books, and motivating audio programs. Most motivational material directly addresses the way you think. Much of the motivational or "positive thinking" material aims to bring back your determination — to help you believe you aren't helpless — that you *can* accomplish your goal.

One of the ways the writers of "success books" help you believe you can achieve your goal is by telling true stories of people who had worse setbacks than you (sometimes much worse) and who had bigger goals than you (sometimes far bigger) but who somehow achieved them.

Hearing these kinds of stories puts your own goals and setbacks into perspective enough to eliminate your feelings of helplessness. It makes you correct your opinion of your own ability.

If you have been disheartened, reading these stories can make you consider the possibility that you're not incapable after all. Maybe your dream is not impossible to achieve after all. Your motivation resurges. And *because* you feel motivated, you get off your butt and get back to work with determination.

And what do you know? Usually the motivational writers were *right* — you really *had* misperceived the hopelessness of your situation! You weren't helpless after all! *You can if you believe you can,* they say, which is really another way of saying that *your belief that you can't is mistaken.* And that is almost always a true statement.

Think about the significance of this. If you actually achieve your goal, then your belief that you couldn't was a *cognitive distortion*, a mistaken notion, an unreasonable and premature assumption.

Motivational material is considered by many to be "bootstrapping." That is, the whole enterprise is fake. It is merely giving people false hopes. You can't pick yourself up by your own bootstraps. Can you? But the accusation falls on deaf ears because in fact, it works. Thousands of very successful people will acknowledge motivational material as being pivotal to their success.

Motivational stuff *is* a kind of bootstrapping in the sense that what allowed those people to overcome their "impossible" obstacles wasn't anything more than their own belief that they could. The human will is a powerful force and once someone has definitely made up their mind that they can and will achieve something no matter what, they often find a way. Determination gets those creative juices flowing, and "unsolvable" problems get solved.

Another way to look at it, however (besides as a kind of bootstrapping), is that the original belief (that the goal was impossible) was *false*. The original belief was unrealistically pessimistic.

In other words, the person who had previously believed the goal was impossible had irrationally jumped to a conclusion without sufficient evidence and held the conclusion with unjustifiable certainty. He underestimated his own ability. Or he overestimated the obstacles in his way.

SUCCESS THROUGH PMA

I think the motivational material of Brian Tracy, Napoleon Hill, Earl Nightingale, and others like them have been under-acknowledged and underused by academics and therapists as legitimate tools for overcoming feelings of defeat.

Let's take Napoleon Hill as an example. His work focuses on removing hopelessness and helplessness by making you realize the *benchmark state* can become your *actual state* with sufficient determination, and that your degree of determination is within *your* power to change (with autosuggestion, for example). His work focuses on the most important cause of defeat: The belief that the cause of a setback is *permanent.*

This same factor is also an important component of Martin Seligman's work, and one of the elements of David Burns' work. When you decide the cause of a setback is permanent, it takes the wind out of your sails. It removes your fighting spirit. You feel defeated, depressed, or demoralized, whether your goal is getting rich or getting married or feeling happy. You feel defeated, you feel your goal is hopeless. So you give up.

And yet, if you are able to argue with your defeatist thoughts, you can often renew your willingness to persist, and that often turns the tide. You start achieving results. The results reinforce your belief that you are *not* helpless and your situation is *not* hopeless. It creates an upward spiral of accomplishment and motivation.

In other words — to put it in Julian Simon's model — you have a benchmark state you want to achieve. But you think your actual state (several setbacks in a row, for example) makes the benchmark impossible to achieve. Both Seligman and Hill address this issue, but in different ways.

For example, say your benchmark is to have a good relationship with someone who loves you.

That's your goal. But your actual state, as far as you are concerned, is that you have just been divorced and your ex-spouse said really harsh things to you, so you feel unlovable and you think nobody could ever love you. But you want with all your heart to love and be loved. The actual state and the benchmark state are so far apart, it makes you depressed. You feel defeated. You don't think your goal is really possible.

Burns might say, "You are not correct about your unlovability. If you corrected your assessment, you would realize it is possible someone could love you. Then you might act differently, treat yourself and others differently, and because of that difference, you may be able to achieve the benchmark state." Burns would help you find what specific mistakes you're making in your thinking, like overgeneralizing or jumping to hasty conclusions.

Seligman might say, "It is not necessarily true that you are *permanently* unlovable. Perhaps you could change your behavior so that you were more lovable."

Napoleon Hill would approach this differently. He would tell you to imagine your goal clearly and tell yourself constantly that you can do it, and to take lots of action that will move you toward that goal, no matter what obstacles you run into.

These three different approaches are all trying to accomplish the same thing if you look at motivation and demoralization as two ends of a single scale. Strong motivation is on the high end and depression is on the low end. What the different approaches have in common is attempting to move you up that scale.

One of the most important ways to move up the scale is to keep the level of challenge just right. One way to do that is to correct your mistaken assumption that your goal is out of reach. Another way is to make the goal smaller so it seems more within the reach of your ability. Another way is to convince yourself you can do it even though it feels out of reach. Another way is to increase your *ability* so the goal is less challenging to you.

One of the things all these have in common is they put the accomplishment of the goal within *your own control.* When you feel helpless, you don't feel you have enough ability to control the outcome. If you feel your goal is hopeless, you have decided the goal is too big and you can't control the outcome of it.

A feeling of control — that *you* have a say in how things turn out, and that you're not counting on outside forces to make things happen — is vital to a feeling of motivation.

The life raft saga Dougal Robertson wrote, entitled, *Survive the Savage Sea,* has many illustrations of this principle. For example, after their sailboat was sunk by killer whales and they had been adrift on their raft and dingy for seven days, alone in the vast Pacific ocean, hungry, thirsty, and desperate, they spotted a ship! It was only about three miles away.

Trembling, Dougal hurriedly lit flares, one after the other, and they all yelled and screamed at the top of their lungs, and waved their arms frantically. Dougal even tried to light their little makeshift sail on fire (it only melted), but the ship kept steadily on its course and disappeared on the horizon.

Up until this point, Dougal had been counting on *rescue*. He felt the only chance they had of making it home alive was to be *rescued*. But as he sat there, gulping air, exhausted and profoundly disappointed, something happened to him, he says, "that changed the whole aspect of our predicament. If these poor bloody seamen couldn't rescue us," he wrote later, "then we would have to make it on our own and to hell with them."

Dougal's attitude changed immediately and permanently on the spot. What changed? He put his goals into his own control. To accomplish his goal, he decided, he would *not* rely on the alertness of others or the chance of a ship. He would rely on *himself*.

Dougal wrote, "We would survive without them, yes, and that was the word from now on, 'survival' not 'rescue' or 'help' or dependence of any kind, just survival."

This change in his attitude changed his motivation immediately. "I felt the strength flooding through me," he wrote of this event, "lifting me from the depression of disappointment to a state of almost cheerful abandon."

His change of mind had an immediate consequence. Later that very day, a large sea turtle bumped into their raft. As Dougal says, "The day before, I would have said, 'Leave it, we can't manage that,' but now things were different." If they were to survive until landfall, they would need to eat.

They managed to catch it and haul it aboard, all eighty pounds of it. They badly needed food, and now they had it. But how to slaughter it? "Twenty-four hours previously I would not have had the stomach for such a bloody business..."

But his attitude had changed. He was focused and determined now. They would make it home alive no matter what anyone else did, and he would do whatever was necessary.

The same principle applies to you and your goals, too. Make sure your goal is within *your* control. Concern yourself with what *you* can do, not what others might do or what the weather might do or what the economy might do — it raises your fighting spirit and motivates you to act. It helps to keep the level of challenge just right.

The moment you start to feel the outcome of your goal is not in your control, your motivation will begin to fade. If the achievement of your goal is out of your control it means you feel you either don't have enough skill yet, or no amount of skill would accomplish it. Either way spells doom to your motivation.

SMALL TARGETS

Targets improve performance. Definite purpose does better than indefinite purpose — better in the sense that you perform better, but also better for your health, happiness, and a sense of meaning.

If your purpose is ongoing or long-term, set landmarks or targets. Slavomir Rawicz is a great case in point. He was in a forced labor camp in Siberia after World War II. He and six men escaped from the camp and set a big goal: Make it to India alive. They made the river Lena as their first objective, and felt great satisfaction when they achieved it, even though it was not very far compared to how far they had to go.

Next they aimed for the northern end of Lake Baikal because they knew they could follow it south and it would take them almost out of Siberia.

Lake Baikal is a very long, banana-shaped lake stretching four hundred miles from the northern end to the southern tip.

In this way, one target at a time, they kept their determination strong as they attempted to reach their impossible goal. Each target was a win and gave them a feeling of accomplishment, and it kept their motivation high.

They made their way, incredibly enough, all the way across Siberia, moving south, then across Mongolia and the infamous Gobi Desert, and then all the way across the Himalayas and finally to India, and they did it *on foot*. They were fugitives being pursued by the heartless USSR secret police. They did it with only an ax and a knife. But four of them made it alive to India (it took them a month to cross the Gobi desert and two of the men died in the desert).

Rawicz accomplished his impossible goal one target at a time. If you feel overwhelmed and stressed, concentrate on the smallest unit you can: *This* task, *this* piece of paper. Deal with only this small unit until it is complete. Then choose another small unit. If you look at your purpose and it seems huge and discouraging, focus on the smallest target.

Michael Lotito is in the *Guinness Book of World Records* for eating an airplane. Doesn't that sound impossible? He did it by grinding the whole airplane into a fine powder, and then adding a little to his meals every day.

Break something into small enough units and even a huge task becomes quite easy. You might think, *I can't eat an airplane!*

But you *can* swallow this little teaspoon of grit in a glass of water.

Break your purpose down into targets. Make a list of targets, put them in order, and then get to work, accomplishing those targets one after the other until you have succeeded.

And keep your attention on what you *can* do. If your thoughts stray to what *can't* be done or what you feel is impossible, the level of perceived challenge will rise too high, causing you to lose your motivation.

In all these ways, you can cultivate and strengthen your motivation by keeping the level of challenge just right.

Measure Your Progress

IN A STUDY of professional soccer players from several different countries, the players showed a consistent pattern: A high percentage of them were born at a time that allowed them to be a little older than their peers. In other words, let's say the school year starts in September and you were born in December. You're supposed to start kindergarten at five years old, so do you start school when you are almost five, or do you wait a whole year till you're almost six?

My brother and sister were both in this situation. My sister started early, so throughout her time in school, she was just a little younger than most of her peers. My brother started late so he was always older than most his peers, and it made a difference. He was always a little more developed, a little further along in his physical growth than most of his classmates.

The study of soccer players showed that most of the players who are good enough to become professionals started school a little older than most of their peers because their birthday was in the middle of the school year.

What does this have to do with motivation? Because they started a little late, they were more physically developed than their peers. So when they played sports, they did better than their peers, and the success motivated them.

Success is motivating. Winning is motivating.

One of the most important reasons for making a list and putting it in order is to break the task into small enough pieces that you can experience successes. Those little wins boost your motivation. You can see and feel you're making progress toward your ultimate goal. You're winning. And that is motivating.

One of the most important reasons for managing your challenge (so you stay within the "just right" range) is so you can experience successes, because that will spur you on, arouse your interest, and keep you motivated.

This is all fine and well, but we've got a problem. The brain has a negative bias and reality has a negative bias (of course, reality has no bias, but it functions as if it does). When you're succeeding but make one little mistake, guess what your mind will fixate on? The mistake, of course.

That's why you must measure your progress. Figure out some way to measure your progress so you can counteract the negative bias (keeping you from feeling demoralized by mistakes), and so you can see yourself succeeding (because it raises your motivation).

How do you measure progress? Simple. Take the most important result, mark it on a chart, and post it. For example, I've tried several measurements with my writing and found the best one is simply hours spent writing.

I once measured "pages written" because I'd learned many famous writers did it that way. They would set a goal of writing *fifty pages a day* or something like that. But when I did that, I would hurry through the task and be verbose, like I used to do in high school when I didn't feel like writing but had a "word count" quota.

Now I measure just the hours I spend, and it works really well. You might think I'd just sit there and use up time, but I never have. I am motivated to write the book or article or whatever, so I end up concentrating fully on the writing. I even found that measuring writing time had an extra advantage because I take my time with the editing, and improve it a lot because I took the time. I could take all the time I wanted. I was "being paid by the hour." It's the best measurement to chart for me.

So find one result you can measure. And of course, the result you choose makes a difference. Experiment and see what gives you the results you want, and then put your chart where you can see it. It might be hours per week, number of cold calls, number of resumes mailed out per month. Chart it and post it. Keep it up to date.

Your posted progress becomes a *visible* success, and success is motivating.

ALREADY-DONE LIST

Another method I use is keeping a backward to do list. This is a different way to solve the problem we talked about before: The disheartening feeling that you've worked all day with nothing to show for it.

How many times have you stayed busy all day, but at the end of the day, had the disconcerting feeling that you haven't really done anything? This makes your actions feel futile and pointless. All that work, all day long, and it feels like you did *nothing* worthwhile. This is demotivating, of course.

How can this even be possible? I wonder if a hunter-gatherer felt that way? I don't think so. At the end of the day, she's got a pile of nuts or a dead deer to show for her efforts. Does a brick-layer ever feel like her actions are futile? Doubt it.

When she started the day, the wall was only two feet high. Now it is eight feet high.

What I'm driving at here is that the problem is not you. It's the tasks. The modern world is full of invisible, hard-to-remember activities — banking online, for example. And these activities are not in any way futile or unimportant. They can be very important. But they aren't *visible*. Once you finish your banking task, you close your computer, and what happens? Your desk, your world, looks exactly as it did before you started as if nothing happened.

Now that we can start to see what the problem is, a solution begins to seem obvious: Make a list.

You can make a list of what you will do ahead of time, or you can make a list of what you've already done as soon as you finish it, sort of like making a to-do list backwards.

So as soon as you finish your banking, write on a piece of paper, "did the banking." Maybe even put a checkmark next to it. Do the dishes, then write it down and checkmark it. Keep this up all day, and then — and this is the most important part — before you go to bed, *read your list*. It doesn't take very long to do, and it gives you three positive benefits:

1. You will no longer feel your actions are futile. You won't be disheartened by the

sense that you're spinning your wheels and getting nowhere.

2. You will feel more motivated. When you see you are, in fact, getting things done, some of which are important to your goals, you are motivated to do even more.

3. You will find out how you spend your time. You will improve the way you use your time without even really trying. At the end of the day you'll look at your list and you'll see a lot of things you've spent part of your day doing were a waste of time. You may be unaware of just how much time you waste, because those activities have been as invisible as your productive tasks.

Make a done list every day, adding to it every time you complete even the smallest task, and at the end of the day, read it over. This is a simple way to measure your progress. It helps you stay focused and it gives you feedback that indicates your progress, and progress is motivating.

Consume
Motivational Material

I HEARD ZIG ZIGLAR (a well-known motivational speaker) say something once that has stuck with me: The reason motivation fades is that the world is full of demotivators. The naysaying of friends, the problems that come up, the constant distractions, the temptations to go off track, etc. And of course, the worst demotivators of all are what we do in our own heads.

Alan Bean, one of the twelve astronauts who walked on the moon, said he listened to motivational tapes in his car on the way to his NASA training while he was preparing for his space flight.

The Apollo astronauts were the most confident, competent, healthy people on the planet. They had passed severe physical and psychological tests to even qualify for the program, and then were trained intensely. It might seem surprising that Bean would listen to tapes to increase his motivation, but one of the reasons he made it into the space program is that he knew how to keep himself motivated and focused. Listening to motivational material in the car is one very effective way to do that.

Most of us are aware that working toward a big goal is where the fun is, but motivation *doesn't seem to last*. People go to seminars and hear motivational speakers and get excited about their goals and their lives, but the motivation and excitement fades. What we need is a way to *stay* motivated — not faking it, not forcing ourselves, but *really* feeling motivated. Listening to motivational material fulfills this need very efficiently.

Motivational material all basically says the same thing: Set goals, concentrate your effort and attention, persist, and make good use of your time. The most important thing it does is make you think about what you want. It puts your attention on your goal and convinces you it is possible.

Motivational material often contains stories of people overcoming obstacles to achieve their goals — obstacles much worse than the obstacles you face, and goals much bigger than yours. The result is that you feel you can do it if you apply yourself.

The most important thing you can do for long term success is *keep your attention on what you want.*

This is difficult to do. You naturally think up other goals and you naturally fixate your attention on what is *in the way* of what you want. But motivational material makes it much easier to keep your attention on what you want.

Really, *anything* you do that helps you stay motivated is good. Motivational material just happens to be especially designed for it.

Your greatest achievements — the things you've done in your lifetime that mean the most to you — were difficult. The only reason you did them was that you were sufficiently motivated.

That strong motivation wasn't a *fluke*. It wasn't random. You don't have to wait for that kind of motivation to descend on you at the whim of the gods. You can nurture and cultivate and enhance and heighten your motivation to an astonishing degree. And the most direct way to do it is with motivational material.

A lot of people who become successful attribute their persistence in the face of setbacks to motivational material.

Mary Kay Ash of the Mary Kay cosmetics empire told Zig Ziglar she would never get into her car without an audio recording she could listen to while she was driving.

H.L. Hunt, who was worth three billion dollars by the end of his life, was a big fan of motivational recordings.

What I'm saying is as simple as it sounds. If you've ever thought, "I'm just not very motivated," or "I can't sustain my motivation for very long," this message is especially for you. You can be as motivated as you want to be. You have not yet explored all the ways you can nurture your own natural motivation.

Saying, "I'm not very motivated but I would like to be," is like saying, "I'm not very dry after a shower but I would like to be." If somebody said that to you, your first response might be, "Have you tried toweling off?" Because of course if a person wants to towel off, it is obviously completely within their power to do so. All they have to do is try.

Same with motivation. It is completely within your power to be as motivated as you want to be. But of course you have to try.

Just to give you a little extra motivation to listen to audio recordings while you drive, a study by the University of Southern California found that if you live in a city and drive 12,000 miles a year, you can get the equivalent of a two-year college education every three years by listening to audiobooks while you drive.

One thing they didn't study is that the listeners are likely to experience less stress or frustration while driving than non-listeners. Why? Because the listeners are doing something they *want* to do rather than feeling helpless and frustrated about being stuck in traffic and unable to do what they want to be doing. Sitting there stuck in traffic is not a complete waste of your valuable time if you use it to learn something you want to learn.

It's easier to learn something really well when you listen in your car because you're more likely to listen to an audiobook several times than you are to read a book several times, and repetition is the key to retaining information.

In a study on memory, researchers found that when people listened to information they'd never heard before, two weeks later they could only re-member *two percent* of it. But if they listened to it on six consecutive days, they remembered *sixty-two percent* of it two weeks later. Repeated listening is an effective way to learn.

Wallace Johnson, one of the co-founders of Holiday Inns International, even at eighty years old, still listened to motivational material every day. He was one of the first to do so. Back before they had books recorded by professional readers, he had one of his employees read nonfiction books onto tapes for him.

"The reason many people don't succeed or are unhappy," wrote Johnson, "is that they have sour, negative, resentful attitudes." In his speeches, he always tried to emphasize what he believed was the most important thing in life: "the development of the proper attitude."

One good way to develop a better attitude is to listen to motivational material in your car.

Motivation fades only if you stop motivating yourself. You can't get motivated once and expect it to last a lifetime. That would be like being nice to your spouse once and expecting your marriage to be blissful for the rest of your life. It doesn't work that way. It would be like trying to exercise once and being disappointed you don't stay in shape. It would be like watering a plant once and wondering why it eventually wilted. You get the idea.

Whether or not you stay motivated is completely up to you, and it requires as much "work" as any other worthwhile state you're trying to maintain — a state of harmony between you and your mate, a state of health for your body, a state of ease in your life. They all require sustained action to maintain.

The good news is that it isn't really "work" because the benefits so far outweigh the cost in terms of effort. You get *immediate* rewards for your effort to stay motivated — you get to feel motivated, and that's a wonderful way to go through the day. And then you also get the rewards that come from all the work you were motivated to do.

The content of your mind determines whether you feel motivated or not, and listening to motivational material is an excellent form of training for what to say to yourself.

Recordings of good motivational speakers can help you learn how to stay motivated and focused on your purposes. For example, when I was going from bookstore to bookstore to convince them to carry my first book, I listened to a tape on selling that said, "it doesn't matter whether this customer buys anything. It is the process of going out and calling on people that does the trick. Any particular call is unimportant." I used that idea in my self-coaching when I was visiting bookstores. Instead of getting anxious about this particular bookstore and whether or not they'd say yes, instead of feeling disappointed if they said no, I relaxed and reminded myself it is the *process* of going to bookstores that works, regardless of what *this* bookstore did. Listening to that tape on selling trained me to think differently, and that helped my attitude.

Listen to motivational material enough and certain phrases will become *memorized*, coming back to you when you need to hear them. Listen to motivational material for *an infusion of motivation*, an enhancement of your focus, and a reminder of important principles.

Motivation is nothing to take lightly. The outcome of your goals depends *almost entirely* on how motivated you are. Here are some classic motivational audioprograms I recommend:

The Science of Personal Achievement: The 17 Universal Principles of Success by Napoleon Hill

The Psychology of Achievement by Brian Tracy
Lead The Field by Earl Nightingale

Goals: Setting And Achieving Them On Schedule by Zig Ziglar

The Psychology of Winning by Denis Waitley

Psycho-Cybernetics by Maxwell Maltz and Dan Kennedy

They all basically say the same thing: Choose good goals, stay focused on them, imagine the way you want things to go, take plenty of action, and talk to yourself in a way that maintains a strong feeling of motivation and confidence. You can't hear this enough!

Some give bonus tips. But perhaps even more important than the *information* they give you is that while you're listening, you're thinking about your goal. That is the most motivating thing you can do. And they tell you stories about people who overcame setbacks. That helps prevent you from becoming demoralized by your own setbacks.

It doesn't matter that they all say basically the same thing. After listening ten times, you might not want to hear it again. But if you want to keep motivating yourself, you can listen to a book by a *different* author and even though he may say roughly the same thing, it's a different voice and he's saying it in a different way using different illustrations, so you'll enjoy listening. And it will re-motivate you because it makes you think about your goal.

The fact that many of us spend a considerable amount of time driving alone can be a wonderful opportunity to increase our knowledge and keep ourselves motivated. Don't waste this valuable opportunity.

RUDY'S PERSISTENCE

I love the movie, *Rudy*. It's a true story about a boy who wants to play football for Notre Dame even though he's small, not very strong, not very quick, doesn't have the money for college (and neither do his parents), and gets lousy grades in high school.

But because of his formidable persistence and consistently great attitude, because of his willingness to keep moving toward his goal no matter what obstacles barred his way, he actually achieved his goal. It is truly inspiring to watch.

The real Rudy Ruettiger was a consultant for the movie, and made sure the movie was an accurate depiction of his life. But it leaves out some interesting facts. You can't put a whole life into one movie without omitting *something*.

One of the things the movie left out is what I consider to be a vital part of the story: *How* he became so incredibly persistent. That is the characteristic of Rudy's that stands out the most in the movie. Rudy persisted long past the point when most other people would have thrown in the towel.

Luckily, Rudy wrote about his experience in more detail, so we know the answer. A particular event changed his life. He consumed some motivational material.

In the movie (and in real life), only one person supported Rudy's dream to play football for Notre Dame — his best friend, Pete. When Pete died in a tragic accident, something happened to Rudy, and he realized if he was going to make his dream happen, he'd better get on with it, because life is short.

A few days later he was in a bookstore and found a paperback copy of *Psycho-Cybernetics*. "I took the book home and read it cover to cover," says Rudy, "and then I started again at the beginning."

The book made a profound impression on Rudy, and he immediately started acting on his newfound understanding of how goals are accomplished.

"Although I was already 23, I immediately headed for Notre Dame with the attitude, 'I'm going to do this, period, end of sentence,' and new opportunities were created just by me showing up."

I've had similar experiences where my commitment to a goal — all by itself — seemed to make things happen, almost like magic. You probably have too.

"Maltz said if you take action, the plan will unfold in front of you," wrote Rudy. "You can develop your game plan as you move toward your goal. Sometimes it's better not to have everything all laid out; focusing too much on how you think it should go can cause you to miss opportunities."

According to Rudy, the book changed his life.

If you have important goals (and I'll bet you do) find yourself a copy of *Psycho-Cybernetics* and read it. It's one of the best self-help books ever written.

Two things make the book exceptional: First, it's easy to read. Second, it is *complete*. It talks about the value of setting goals and how to set goals, and how to visualize your goals to make them real. But it also talks about one of the most important barriers to achievement: Your self-image.

If you have a goal but believe you're a loser, no matter how hard you try, you will not be able to accomplish your goal. Something will always cause you to fail before you reach it.

If this has been happening to you, dig into the self-image psychology in Maltz's book and follow the practical suggestions for eliminating the internal barriers to your success. Rudy said, "I learned from *Psycho-Cybernetics* that it's all in what you think."

But that doesn't mean "just think positive thoughts and everything will turn out well." There is more to it. Maltz goes into detail about exactly how to use your mind effectively to overcome the psychological obstacles to achievement.

Rudy wrote, "Every one of us uses our mind to create our life. My story can be your story — if you are willing to swim against the stream, fight against the odds, and believe you can be whatever you want to be.

The content of your mind in the present is all-important. Listening to motivational material is a very easy way to control and direct the content of your mind.

Take Time to Think

I FELT DISHEARTENED because my back hurt from sitting so long at the computer, and since I was writing my book on the computer, it seemed I had the option of either being in pain, or not working. But I really wanted to work. That was frustrating.

It occurred to me I also did lots of *other* stuff on the computer, and if I stopped doing *those*, my back might not hurt. I tried it and it worked.

I came up with this insight, and most of the good ones I've ever come up with, by thinking. Before you dismiss that as too obvious to even mention, please hear me out.

If you have a problem or difficulty, or you feel confused, or you just feel like you've been working-working-working without a break, take some time and do nothing.

Let yourself think about whatever comes into your mind. Don't just give yourself ten minutes for this. Go a half hour at least, and preferably longer, because it takes the mind a little while to settle down. Go for a leisurely walk through a quiet area, or sit still in a quiet place and just sit there.

I call it this "T5" (for take the time to think). The following suggestions will make your T5 productive:

1. Take *enough* time. Imagine you want to tell me something and you're not sure how to say it, and I repeatedly *interrupt* you to say, "Come on, come on, I don't have all day!" Imagine what that would be like and you'll realize it's hard to be creative or even intelligible under circumstances like that. The mind functions better when it's not under pressure. This is just as true with thinking as it is with talking. So give yourself *time* to T5. I usually set a timer and make myself sit there until the timer goes off. That way I don't hurry myself through it. I know I have plenty of time, and I do not try to hurry up and think so I can get up sooner.

2. Have paper and pen handy. You will get ideas. You'll think of things you want to take care of. Write these down so you don't have to use part of your mind trying to remember something. You will often spend almost all of your thinking time writing, and that's perfectly okay. Writing is an excellent way to think. That's why people benefit from "journaling." Writing down your thoughts and feelings is a form of T5 and it is very therapeutic. But in this case, you're not trying to write a lot (but you're not preventing yourself from writing a lot). The purpose of having paper and pen handy is to keep your mind unencumbered by things you are trying to remember. So if you think, "Oh, I need to pay rent tomorrow," write it down so you free up your mind. You don't want to use up part of your attention trying to remember that. You'll also probably get insights you'll want to remember later. Write those down too.

3. T5 in an undistracting environment. Don't try to think when you can hear or watch a television or music. If you go for a walk, walk in the least distracting place you can, preferably through the woods or across an empty desert or through a quiet neighborhood where you're not going run into someone you know.

4. Keep it uninterrupted. You know how hard it would be to carry on a conversation with someone bursting through the door every five minutes to interrupt? You would keep losing your train of thought. Same with T5. As the minutes tick by, your mind settles down and begins to think. *Every time* you're interrupted, your mind has to settle down again afterward, and sometimes you won't find that train of thought again.

The best way is to sit down in a quiet place alone. Set your timer for one hour, and just sit there. I've done this hundreds of times and it calms me every time. Stress melts away. It clarifies what I'm up to. I solve problems that have been bothering me in the back of my mind.

I am often surprised that my mind seems to have a backlog of things to think about. Because I go from one activity to another and most of them use my mind, I don't normally have any time to think about things, so the "unthought" things are somehow stashed away for thinking about later. I don't purposely do this. It just seems to happen by itself.

As soon as I sit down, my mind goes to work, almost like the maintenance program on my computer. My computer is set so if it is inactive for thirty minutes, the computer automatically starts an antivirus scan. The computer has been waiting for an idle period to clean things up.

The mind seems to be like that too. As soon as your mind starts to settle down, as soon as it realizes you're not involved in anything, it starts to clear things up. Little questions that have been nagging you come to the foreground and get worked out. It sounds so boring to just sit still for an hour, but it is very calming to sort things out, figure things out, think things out. You'll feel wonderfully clearheaded when you're done.

You might think that only a "contemplative type of person" would find this enjoyable. Maybe you think only introspective people can do it. But I'm not an introspective person at all. I'm normally energetic and dislike sitting still. I have to *make* myself sit still, but when I do, and when my mind starts to get past the boredom, good things start happening. Try it a few times before you make up your mind about it.

BESIEGING A PROBLEM

One way to T5 is just to let your mind think, without trying to think about anything in particular. You will find your mind thinking about things you need to think about, and that works great.

But another good way is to deliberately concentrate on a specific problem. Often a problem will yield to sustained and concentrated thinking. More often than not.

Think of this kind of T5 as a "Mongol siege." When Genghis Khan (no relation) wanted to attack and defeat a walled city, he would choose a particular section of the city wall and begin the siege. One third of his army would attack that spot for eight hours, to be immediately replaced by another third of the army attacking that same spot for another eight hours, etc. The siege went on, twenty-four hours a day until the city fell.

And it always fell.

"The sheer relentlessness of the Mongol siege," wrote Brian Tracy, "was so devastating that no city ever withstood it."

If you have a problem or challenge, and you thought about it and concentrated on it, and you didn't give up, can you see you would probably find a solution every time?

And in case you want to accuse me of over-stating my case, let me be clear I'm not saying any person can solve every problem that ever existed. I'm not talking about cold fusion here or ending world hunger. I'm talking about specific problems *you* have — problems that are stumping you or demoralizing you — problems you ran into on the way to your goal.

If you concentrate your mind on your problem or challenge, and don't either give up in despair or jump wildly onto the first idea that pops into your head, but instead give it some serious, sustained thought, either on a walk or sitting quietly for an hour or two at a time, can you see you would probably overcome every obstacle — either solving the problem outright, or finding a way to skirt around it?

Do it like a Mongol siege. Be relentless. Keep thinking about it, even after you have already come up with some good ideas. See if you can think up an even *better* idea.

Here's how to generate ideas to solve a problem or accomplish a purpose: Make a list on paper. Set a goal ahead of time for how many ideas you'll come up with, and don't stop until you hit that target. This will prevent you from stopping with the first good idea. Always try to think of something better.

Try alternatives in your head to see how they'd work.

A hard-thinking session that didn't produce a single good idea was still worthwhile. It planted the question deep in your mind. Your mind will keep working on it.

Coming up with ideas primarily consists of asking a question over and over no matter how many good answers you've already gotten.

This is a lot like meditation: Your mind drifts away and you keep coming back to the question. One of the most practical, universally applicable principles I've ever used is: Accumulate quantity and then sort.

First, clarify the problem. Take your time on this first step. Try to define a problem clearly and be very specific and as accurate as you can. Then generate a list of possible solutions. Strain your brain on this one. Don't settle for the few obvious answers that come to mind easily. Dig. Then pick the best solution. Keep in mind that creativity and selection are two different functions and need to be separated. First come up with ideas. *Then* judge and compare them, and choose the best one. Don't do any judging and comparing while you're coming up with ideas.

THE PRINCIPLE IS SIMPLE

Take the time to think. Let your mind sort things out. If you feel upset by something, you can find your inner peace by taking the time to think. You can just keep thinking and writing and walking in all your spare time until you are no longer upset — until you either feel fine or feel so motivated you want to get up and get busy on some of these ideas you've thought up.

Do you think you don't have time for this? How much time do you spend watching TV and movies? Can you take some time from that? A movie usually takes two hours. That's a big chunk of uninterrupted time. How much time do you spend on the internet?

One of the odd facts about T5 is that it can't be done lying down. You have to sit up or walk. When you lie down, your mind switches to a dreamy mode where keeping your attention on anything in particular becomes difficult, and you tend to daydream or fall asleep.

I've read a lot about meditation. And one surprising fact is held in common by all of them — Japanese Zen meditation, Hindu Yoga meditation, American Silva Mind Control meditation, etc. — all of them spend an inordinate amount of time talking about what seems a very mundane and nitpicky topic: your posture while meditating. You're supposed to keep your back straight, your hands just so, head at such-and-such an angle. The different kinds of meditation may have different postures, but they *all* tell their practitioners very clearly how to sit. And no matter how different they all seem, they all aim for an upright, stable posture.

And I've found that's also best for T5. A slumping, kicking-back posture will make it almost impossible to remain alert and think clearly.

TIME-PRESSURE IS UNNATURAL

Time with *nothing to do* is necessary for good mental health. Ponder this for a moment: Do you have a lot of great childhood memories? Does it seem like you had a lot of fun back then? Have you ever wondered what you had then that you don't have now?

Think about it. What did you have then that you don't have now that would contribute to having more fun?

You know what I think it is? You had time with nothing to do. And you know what? You did not want it or like it, even though it contributed to your happiness.

Just as we have more carbohydrates available to us than is natural, constantly tempting us with foods we aren't adapted to eat in great quantities, our visual and auditory world constantly tempts us with more stimulation that we have evolved to handle well.

Quiet time with *nothing happening* is the natural remedy. Whenever I have spent an hour or more doing this, I have always ended feeling profoundly calm and relaxed. My mind feels uncluttered and at peace.

It takes a little while to settle down. For fifteen minutes, sometimes twenty, your mind will be restless. You will feel bored. You'll have a craving to *do* something. But then your mind will start to relax and sort things out, all by itself.

If you find that after a half hour you are simply obsessing about a worry and getting nowhere, you can switch to besieging the problem, concentrating on solving a single problem (the one that's bothering you the most).

I've sometimes felt as if I've found what everyone is searching for — a path to peace of mind. In the aftermath of my newfound clarity and peace, I want to tell everyone about this great invention of mine. But of course, it isn't my invention. It is probably the oldest self-help method there is.

Take the time to think. There's nothing to it. Your mind will naturally do it. The only hard part is making yourself take the time. And you *do* have to *make* yourself. You always have some work to do, or something you feel you ought to be doing, or some TV program you want to watch, or kids to play with or a spouse to talk to, or any of a hundred other interesting, appealing things you want to do besides just sitting there.

Just as we are naturally drawn to eating sweets, we are naturally drawn to filling our attention with stimulation. But it is *calming* to restrain that impulse occasionally.

You know how difficult it is to get anywhere in a conversation when you're constantly interrupted. The same is true for dialog with yourself. You have some things you need to think through, but you are *so continuously distracted*, you're accumulating unresolved issues in the back of your mind. I think this leads to extra stress hormones. That's probably why T5 is so calming.

I once believed that the feeling of being grounded and unfrantic and deeply peaceful could only come from a spiritual or religious or mystical experience. But T5 produces it very reliably.

Gandhi, Lincoln, Emerson — and many other (maybe all) great (and wise and accomplished) leaders spent an unusual amount of time doing nothing but thinking.

Decide ahead of time how long you will think, and stick to it. I suggest *an hour*. Do nothing. Don't knit or whittle or floss your teeth. Make *brief* notes, and nothing more.

When should you T5? Whenever you feel unmotivated about your goal. When you don't know what to do next. When you feel confused, anxious, depressed, frustrated, or unclear. When you have a problem you want to solve.

T5 can bring you peace of mind, but what does that have to do with motivation? When you solve a problem, you increase your motivation. The problem was an obstacle on your way to your goal, and you solved it. When things are nagging you in the back of your mind — things you need to think through — it can be upsetting, frustrating or discouraging. When you clear up those nagging issues, you feel better because you removed obstacles, and that helps you feel more motivated.

T5 is really a core activity, the key, the secret. Purposefulness is clarified by thinking. Optimism is attained in thought. You can have what you want in life (peace of mind, successful accomplishment, great relationships) if you take the time to think often enough.

Do you want peace of mind? Clarity? A feeling of being grounded and centered? A feeling of certainty about what you're doing? A clear sense of direction? All you have to do is take the time to think.

Refresh Your Goals

THE MOST EFFECTIVE way to renew your motivation is to seriously consider giving up on your goal — not as a trick, but sincerely. Oddly enough, this can be extremely motivating. Why? Because it brings you back to reality. After all, this is *your* goal. This is not something you *have to* do; it's something you *want* to do.

But too often a goal you are initially very enthusiastic about and want very badly becomes a drudging chore you feel you *have to* do. Why does this happen?

When you first create a goal, you see the big picture — you see what you want to achieve — and you feel motivated.

Then comes the work. You make your list of things to be done in order to accomplish the goal. You realize it could take many years. You get to work on it, and of course, you hit setbacks. You get bogged down in details. You get bored with tedious parts. You run into problems. And you might even forget why you wanted the goal in the first place.

Your motivation wanes because your attention is no longer on the goal, no longer on what you want. Your attention is on the issues you're dealing with and on what you feel you have to do.

So it's a good idea to refresh your goals once in awhile. Do a mental reboot. Start by seriously considering the possibility of giving up on your goal. Ask yourself, "Do I still want this goal?"

Every once in awhile, when you ask this question, you will find that in fact, you no longer want it — not because of demoralization, but because your values have changed, or you have thought of something better, or you have gotten some new information, or whatever.

But most of the time, once you think about it and give yourself the freedom to give it up and start something new, you'll find you still want your goal.

That realization, all by itself, can make you feel a sudden surge of motivation because now you do not feel you *have to* accomplish your goal. Now you are freshly and vividly aware you sincerely *desire* it, and that's a totally different feeling.

ONLY A PREFERENCE

One of the first principles of the late cognitive-therapy pioneer Albert Ellis was to "upgrade your *musts* to preferences." That is essentially what you do when you allow yourself the freedom to give up on your goal. Ellis uses the principle in therapy because it brings people back to reality, it makes them saner, it restores their mental health.

In *reality*, most of the things you feel you have to do are things you actually simply *prefer* to do (given the consequences one way or the other). But the feeling of wanting to do something is positive and pleasant, while feeling you *must* do something feels like drudgery.

So when Ellis did his therapy, he helped his clients realize some of the musts and shoulds that ran their lives were merely preferences they *themselves* had chosen. This, all by itself, removed a lot of craziness from their lives. It got rid of unnecessary negative emotions.

To give up your goal, to even *consider* giving it up, and then choosing it anew reminds you that your goal is a preference. It really isn't something to feel burdened by.

Someone might say, "No, I really have to, because if I don't, I can't make the mortgage." But this is not entirely accurate. He does, in fact, have the option of selling his house and living in a small apartment.

"I can't do that!" he says, "I have my wife and kids to think about." But the truth is, he really could. And oddly enough, if there was something he wanted badly enough, his wife and kids would probably be willing to sacrifice luxuries for him.

But the point is, you often have many choices you are unaware of. You have choices you haven't thought of. Why? Because you haven't thought about it! You set your goal a long time ago, and now you've got your nose to the grindstone. You need to rise above your project once in awhile and look at the whole picture.

If you think about it, if you look at the whole picture, you may go back to the grindstone, but you'll feel good about it now. You'll realize you have *chosen* it. You will have the alternatives to compare it to fresh in your mind. And you will feel motivated. You'll feel better and get more done.

SAME GOAL, DIFFERENT APPROACH

Sometimes you may feel like giving up because what you're doing isn't working. One alternative to giving up on the goal entirely is to keep the goal but change your approach. For example, remember

I tried to lose weight but was unsuccessful? I thought, "I can't seem to do it."

But now I understand that *the way* I was trying didn't work. The goal was possible after all, but the method I was using was doomed to failure, like trying to criticize someone into a good mood or trying to cure anemia by bloodletting. The philosophy of low-fat, high-carb dieting doesn't work without a lot of self-discipline or social support.

In an historical example of this principle, a group of Norwegians were able to stop Hitler's quest for nuclear weapons by continually changing their approach.

Hitler badly wanted the atom bomb. But first he needed "heavy water" (deuterium oxide, D_2O). Heavy water is like H_2O but the hydrogen is replaced by deuterium atoms (which has two extra neutrons so it is heavier than ordinary water).

After Germany invaded and occupied Norway, Hitler used a facility there to begin the work. Making heavy water required an enormous amount of equipment, and it took a long time to get a sufficient amount, as the heavy water dripped slowly to fill up the tanks.

The Allies found out about this project, and of course, wanted to stop it. The British proposed bombing the heavy-water plant, but it was so close to a town (Vemork), the Norwegian resistance fighters talked them out of it. It would create too many civilian casualties.

They still had the goal (stop Hitler from developing the atom bomb) but their approach needed to change. Giving up the goal wasn't an option anyone seriously considered. Hitler with nuclear weapons? It was unthinkable. So they came up with a different approach.

The British launched a commando raid, using silent gliders. But both gliders crashed. The Nazis captured the twenty-three survivors and executed them.

That approach didn't work. The Allies needed another plan. This was one of England's top military priorities because they had good evidence that Germany was close to building an A-bomb. With only *one* such bomb, Hitler could easily wipe out half of London.

Six Norwegian resistance fighters escaped Norway and volunteered for training in England for the mission. To avoid the fate of the last volunteers, they were all issued a rubber capsule of cyanide to pop in their mouths if they were captured. A soldier only had to bite on the capsule, and it would burst. Within three seconds, he would be dead.

The six volunteers learned how to handle explosives, worked out their plan, their timing, they learned to make detonators, studied diagrams of the buildings and of the nearby German military station, etc. This time they would leave nothing to chance. Hitler's project had to be stopped.

The Norwegians parachuted in — and missed their landing spot by twenty miles. They tried to get to the rendezvous point, but were caught in a blizzard. They were supposed to meet four of their fellow saboteurs already in Norway.

When they eventually successfully got inside the building, they set off explosive charges that destroyed the heavy water cells. Success at last!

But the Germans rebuilt it within months. It was obviously high on their priority list also.

This was *tremendously* discouraging and alarming. That several-month delay, however, might've been enough. Nobody was sure. The United States was pressing for bombing the plant — this was too important to be left to luck.

And finally it was done. British and American planes — 388 bombers in all — dropped 828 bombs.

They devastated the plant, but unfortunately one of the places that was not destroyed was where the heavy water cells were stored!

The Germans decided the heavy water they had already made so far was too vulnerable, so they planned to move it to Germany. For the Allies, this was their last chance. They couldn't let the heavy water make it to Germany.

To get the heavy water out of Norway, first it had to be transported by ferry. Norwegian resistance fighters successfully planted explosives on that ferry, sending it (and all the heavy water) to the bottom of the lake. This was finally the end of Germany's "nuclear dream."

How many different approaches did they try on this single goal? *Four times* they created a plan, trained for it, mobilized the equipment and men, and executed their plan before they finally succeeded in achieving the goal.

If you find yourself in a similar situation — still wanting the goal but having failed using the approach you first came up with — you have another option besides giving up: You can come up with another way. You can use what you learned in your first failed attempt to wipe the slate clean and begin again, knowing what you now know, to create a new plan *using a different approach*. This is another way to refresh your goal.

WHEN YOU DON'T KNOW WHAT TO DO

Sometimes when you seriously consider giving up on a goal, you can't decide whether you really want to or not. There are so many good reasons and feelings on both sides, you're on the fence. You don't know what you want to do. At times like that, the best answer is finish what you started. When in doubt, finish the job.

It is more efficient. You already have something invested in the project, and you have no better alternative. You may merely be in a temporary funk, and it might be foolish to give up on your goal.

I used to occasionally have what I called a "doubt funk." It usually happened when I was in the middle of a big project and I started thinking there was a better use of my time; maybe I should be doing something different; maybe the project would fail; maybe my destiny lay somewhere else and I was wasting my time.

I never went into a doubt funk *between* projects. I've never had a problem *thinking up* new goals and feeling enthusiastic about them.

But I suppose it was "the grass is always greener" because no matter what I was working on, I could think of other projects that might be a better use of my time. I aborted a lot of perfectly good projects because of it. I still have several half-finished books sitting in my filing cabinets. Lots of projects of different kinds down through the years never saw the light of day because a doubt funk came along and deflated my motivation.

I eventually learned the way to handle doubt funks: Finish the project. That policy will get the most done with the greatest fun over a lifetime.

Half-finished projects are a waste of time. To spend all that time getting something halfway done and then stopping means all the hours spent on the project were wasted. And wasting time is demoralizing.

I got the answer to doubt funks when I read a true story about Dr. Archibald Cronin. When Cronin was 33, he was a doctor in London. Once in awhile, he had a doubt funk, thinking maybe he should specialize in a different kind of medical practice. He worried that what he was doing wasn't good enough.

Cronin eventually developed an ulcer and his doctor prescribed the standard treatment in those days — six months "complete rest in the country on a milk diet."

He went to a small farm outside a village in the Scottish Highlands. After about a week, this very energetic, high-strung man was climbing the walls. His mind was thrashing around for something to do. Then he realized he'd always wanted to write a novel if he "ever found the time." He suddenly realized he had found the time! So he began.

After three months of being engrossed in the project, he sent all his handwritten pages to his secretary to type up for him. When he received his first chapter and read it, he was devastated. It was terrible.

He understood with clarity and certainty that he had no business trying to be a writer. He was defeated, demoralized, and embarrassed.

In his anguish and shame, he threw the whole manuscript into the trash.

Feeling glad and relieved that he had "come to his senses," he went for a walk, where he ran into Angus, the farmer, and stopped to chat, as he often did. When Cronin told Angus what he had just done, Angus was silent for a long time.

Then Angus spoke. "My father ditched this bog all his days and never made a pasture."

He stopped digging and looked at Cronin. "I've dug it all my days and never made a pasture. But pasture or no pasture," said Angus as he pushed the shovel back into the bog, "I canna help but dig. For my father knew and I know that if you only dig enough a pasture can be made here."

Angus kept digging. Doggedly. Relentlessly. Unmercifully.

Cronin stood there watching him, and while he watched he experienced an intense personal crisis and then a revelation.

Cronin saw his situation as the pattern he'd followed all his life: He would start off in a particular direction and never get anywhere because *doubt* would overtake him halfway through it.

And then he saw it as a pattern and revelation not just for himself, but for all of humanity. He wrote later, "In this present chaos, with no shining vision to sustain us, the door is wide open to darkness and despair. The way to close that door is to stick to the job that we are doing, no matter how insignificant that job may be, to go on doing it, and to finish it."

Cronin stomped back to his room and pulled his manuscript out of the trash. He was angry and fiercely determined. He got back to work on the manuscript and would not stop, no matter what kind of doubt or frustration he encountered. He kept working until he finally finished the thing.

He randomly chose a publisher out of a catalog and mailed off the manuscript. He'd finished what he set out to do. *Then* he relaxed and recovered from his ulcer.

Just as he was preparing to head back to London, he received a telegram from the publisher: they were interested. Unbelievably, the manuscript he had once thrown away was published as a novel in 1931 (titled *Hatter's Castle*) and sold *three million* copies. It was even made into a movie.

When you don't know whether to give up a goal or finish it, the answer is the same for you and me as it was for Cronin: Go to work on the current project, determined and resolute, and finish it.

MANAGING THE PROJECT

After you finish your project, *then* think about what you want to do next. On your way to a goal, you will think of other goals. Write down those ideas and file them. Then get back to your current project. When you are finished and you're ready to decide on the next goal, look to your file for ideas.

And make sure you take the time to choose your goal. Carefully weigh the possibilities. Make *your decision* a project. You may be spending a lot of time on your next goal. It is a very important decision. Don't choose carelessly or on a whim. Take your time. Give yourself time to consider your alternatives before you jump in.

And when you periodically refresh your goals, give that some time too. Take the time to consider your goal. Find out if you really want it. Most of the time you'll be surprised to find you really do. That is one of the best ways of all to heighten your motivation.

Give Yourself Positive Feedback

ONE NIGHT I was getting ready for bed and I felt disappointed in myself. It had been a busy day but I didn't feel like I'd done much to advance my goals, and there were a couple of things I did poorly. I didn't want to end the day like that because I felt down, as if my efforts were futile. I hate that feeling. It is so demotivating. On days like that I feel like I'm spinning my wheels and going nowhere. I feel frustrated and don't look forward to tomorrow.

Have you ever felt that way? Have you ever wished you had a way to bring yourself out of it? Well, from now on, you'll have something you can use. I invented a technique that night and I've used it many times since, and it works every time to raise my spirits and make me feel strong again, looking forward to another day.

I asked myself, "What did I do today that was *right?*" As soon as I asked it, I thought of something. Earlier that day I was going to say something in anger, but I held my tongue. "That was a good thing to do," I thought to myself. And I already felt better. I had done at least one thing right.

But I didn't stop there. I asked it again. *What did I do right today?* After only a minute's thought or less, I thought of another one. There were three small items on my desk I had been needing to do and not getting around to, and I got them done. I felt better still. The day wasn't a total loss. Not at all. And even though I did a couple things poorly, I had also done a couple things right, and this made me feel better.

I asked the question again a few more times and went to sleep feeling relaxed and satisfied, looking forward to a new day.

If this technique did nothing more than make me feel better, it would be worthwhile. An improved mood is a definite asset. But the question does something else that may be even more valuable: It makes you look into your day to see which actions you took were the most valuable.

Each right thing you do is something you do voluntarily — you have a choice in whether to do them or not.

By paying special attention to which were the truly *good* choices, you clarify your goals and moral principles. You clarify what you think is good. You clarify what you want more of.

Ask yourself tonight: What did you do today that helped you achieve your most important goals? What did you do right today?

Think of something. Enjoy it for a moment, and then ask the question again. What else? And what else? It's an excellent exercise to help you feel good more often and increase your ability to accomplish your goals.

Stay On Track

ALBERT EINSTEIN and another man were working on a scientific paper, and when they were done, they needed a paper clip. They looked around and found one, but it was bent out of shape. So they started looking around for a tool they could use to bend it back into a usable shape, when they came across a whole box of paper clips.

Einstein immediately took out a good paper clip, and bent it into a tool that he then used to bend the original paper clip back into a usable shape.

His partner said, "What are you doing? We have a whole box of perfectly good ones!"

Einstein's reply was, "Once I'm set on a goal, it becomes difficult to deflect me."

He said later in his life that this little incident characterized him better than any other. It's a silly incident, and a foolish waste of time to bend the paper clip back, but the habit of staying on track is extremely powerful, and fully worth it even if sometimes the habit wastes time foolishly.

This world can easily be looked at as a trap designed to take you off course, whatever course you are on. The world is full of enticing temptations to stray from your path. It's full of catastrophes and annoying circumstances that tend to take you off track. It's full of people who want your attention, your energies, and your money to go somewhere other than down *your* track. Staying on track is a challenge.

The chief obstacle is something inside your body, something built into your genetic makeup — a curiosity that makes the human species the most successful animal on Earth; a greed for what you don't have, what you haven't seen, what you have not done, what you haven't heard. A built-in lust for novelty. Combine that built-in desire to gain new and pleasant experiences with the free-enterprise system, and stir. What do you get? A dizzying land of temptations and distractions.

The world is literally screaming for your attention. Advertisers, salespeople, your friends, your enemies, and your own mother want your attention. They want you to take your attention off your goals and put your attention on *their* goals.

Distraction is the chief obstacle.

It doesn't seem like an obstacle, and that's why it's the toughest to overcome. What does it take to overcome it?

TO TRY AND TO FAIL

Gail Borden thought condensed meat was the wave of the future. It was 1844 and people often died from eating tainted meat. Before refrigeration, people needed ways to keep food from spoiling. Gail experimented and found a way to boil 120 pounds of meat down to ten pounds, making it not only easier to carry, but less likely to spoil.

When the California Gold Rush began, he saw a ready market for his product, and he and his brother Tom built a meat-condensing plant and started cranking out the product.

But of course, the Gold Rush didn't last very long. After it was over, his main source of customers dwindled down to nothing and his business went bankrupt.

"Don't infer I've given up," he told a friend. He knew the process of condensation was valuable, and he was determined to convince other people of it.

After several more years of experimentation, he wrote in a letter to a friend, "Every piece of property I own is mortgaged. I labor fifteen hours a day."

Often success doesn't come easy, especially if you want to make a difference. Gail wasn't just trying to make a living. He could have just gotten a job. He had a vision, if you will: A big, shining vision a hundred feet tall of the value of condensation. He knew it was useful, and he was determined to bring his vision to fruition. He said, "I mean to put a potato into a pillbox, a pumpkin into a tablespoon, the biggest sort of watermelon into a saucer."

You and I may think this is strange. Who can say why a particular person feels compelled to accomplish a particular thing? But it is good that it works out that way because many of the products and ideas and ways of doing things we now take for granted and that contribute to our happiness and ease of living were at one time weird little obsessions of obscure people in the past. They knew their contributions would be useful even when nobody around them thought so. Their contributions were made *only because they persisted.*

Some of the contributions, and this may include yours, would never have been made by any other person if the visionary had given up.

Gail knew a lot about condensation, but apparently he was condensing the wrong thing. He was persistent, but he wasn't a blind fool. He did not keep trying to give people what they didn't want. What *would* they want? What could he condense that would serve humanity? That was the question that kept him awake at night.

He remembered a recent incident aboard a ship he had heard about. Cows were on board to provide fresh milk for the babies on the voyage (again, this was before refrigeration). But the cows took sick and *four babies died* from the tainted milk.

Maybe canned condensed *milk* could be useful. Gail started experimenting and eventually found a way to condense milk without making it taste burnt, and opened a factory.

Farmers, seeing this as a threat, started a campaign against this "unnatural" form of milk.

Keep this in mind: When you are doing something that needs to be done, even if it is all good, and even if your intentions are pure, there will usually be *someone* out there who finds your new thing a threat to an already existing status quo, and they'll try to stop you. They will put up obstacles. What can you do to deal with it? *Stay on track.* Continuous, unrelenting action toward your goal is the answer.

Gail continued, even in the face of the propaganda campaign against his milk, and he almost went belly up *again*. But then the Civil War broke out and the Union army thought Borden's condensed milk was the perfect thing for a field ration

— it was reliable, durable, nutritious, and it wouldn't spoil. His business was saved. After the war, public perception had changed, and his business prospered. Condensed milk was indeed useful, and his company has been providing Borden's Condensed Milk for more than 120 years now.

On his grave, the epitaph reads, "I tried and failed, I tried again and again, and succeeded." Every obstacle eventually yielded to his relentless resolve. Why? Because no matter what happened, *he stayed on track*. He didn't give up, even after bankruptcy. He didn't sell out. He overcame the chief obstacle: Distraction.

PERSISTENCE

Robert B. McCall, Ph.D., of the University of Pittsburgh and his colleagues have kept track of 6,700 people for 13 years. Specifically, they are tracking people who were underachievers in school — people who, according to aptitude tests, had a lot of potential to get good grades, but who, in reality, had low grade-point averages. After 13 years, only about 15% of them had achieved a career success equal to their abilities.

What do they lack? Two things, according to McCall: "persistence in the face of challenge," and they are too self-critical. We deal with the self-critical habit in other places, but the lack of persistence is simply a missing thought-habit. This can be remedied.

You are persistent in the face of challenges if you are *in the habit* of being persistent in the face of challenges, and you are in the habit of persisting if you are in the habit of thinking in ways that make you persistent.

Persistence is an extremely important habit. Think about it. You can't really develop competence at *anything* unless you persist through the rough parts, whether it's playing the piano or doing your job or being a satisfying lover.

Any task you undertake, if it's worth the trouble, will have some challenge in it. Some part of it will be tough. No new abilities can be created without persisting in the face of challenges, even if the main challenge is suffering through the boring repetition of playing scales on the piano.

Ability and therefore accomplishment require persistence. It is probably the most important fundamental skill you must have to create the life you want. Keep coming back to the basic fundamentals. The fancy stuff, the non-fundamentals, aren't worth much if the basics aren't in place.

You will persist if you are motivated (that's what these principles are about) and if you prevent demoralization (that's what *Antivirus For Your Mind* is about).

Develop persistence. That's fundamental to achievement. Very few successful people became successful easily. Most of them had to exercise a good amount of persistence to get there, and the same is almost certainly going to be true for you. For example, *Jonathan Livingston Seagull* was published in 1970. It sold more than seven million copies in America in the first five years, and it is still selling. But when Richard Bach was looking for a publisher, *eighteen* publishers turned down his manuscript.

For some goals, for the really good ones, it will take everything you've got to accomplish it. As a matter of fact, it will take *more* than you've got — you'll have to become more than you are now in order to accomplish it. You'll need to *learn* more than you now know. You'll need to *gain skills* you don't have yet.

UNREMITTING RESOLUTION

Relentless resolve can accomplish what seems impossible. In India there are people called "fakirs," which doesn't mean people who are faking anything. They are people who do something amazing that takes years to master, and they do it as a spiritual discipline.

For example, some fakirs hold a particular pose, like a certain religiously appropriate position, and they just keep holding it. This takes intense resolve, because of course, it becomes uncomfortable after only twenty minutes. So they go as long as they can, and then they rest. And then they go as long as they can again, and they keep alternating like this, holding it longer and longer *until they are permanently frozen* in that posture!

They eventually cannot move at all, even if they wanted to. Their disciples have to wash them and force feed them and carry them to the river like a statue to wash them off.

This is amazing. This unlikely accomplishment demonstrates the impressive power of unremitting resolution.

Personally, I think this particular application of willpower is stupid. There are so many worthwhile goals to accomplish in this world, and these guys have developed their powers of resolve to an inconceivable degree and all they have accomplished is to turn themselves into a *vegetable!?* Come on! But it shows that enough resolve can produce results most of us would consider impossible.

In the *Millionaire Mind* page-a-day calendar, the authors, who have studied millionaires scientifically, tell about one example of *a school bus driver* who was able to send his children to medical school, private colleges, and graduate school, and then he retired with a net worth of three million dollars.

How? Obviously you don't make much money as a school bus driver. He was *consistently* frugal. That was important. But the other part was that being a school bus driver gave him a lot of free time every day, and what he did, consistently — *staying on track* year after year — was read about investments. He saved money by being frugal and then very intelligently and carefully invested his money.

That's how he did it. Not with a supreme exertion but by staying on purpose no matter what the temptations or distractions.

You will be taken off track again and again until you learn to stick with your purpose. With practice, you might get to the level of Einstein's concentration. And when you can focus, you'll be like a laser beam, cutting through obstacles and barriers and flying straight to your objective with power and speed.

Okay, so I've covered nine fundamental principles with which you can cultivate your inner fire of motivation. Use them to keep your motivation burning white hot, and your life will never be the same again.

How to Cultivate Fire

1. Prune your goals.

2. Make a list, put it in order.

3. Keep the level of challenge just right.

4. Measure your progress.

5. Read and listen to motivational material.

6. Take the time to think.

7. Refresh your goals.

8. Give yourself positive feedback.

9. Stay on track.

Behold the
Power of Purpose

The most powerful weapon
on earth is the human soul on fire.

- Marshal Foch

WHEN ALBERT EINSTEIN reached 70, he retired. He had reached his goals, assumed he'd expended his usefulness to the world, and retired. He didn't set any new goals. He became depressed and listless, as people often do when they no longer have a sense of purpose. He stopped taking his dog for walks. Life lost its luster.

Then one day he realized it might not be over; he might still have something to contribute to the world. He decided to do two things:

1. develop a plan to control the destructive use of atomic power

2. to discover peacetime uses for atomic power

He came alive! The luster was back. He took his dog for walks again. He had a purpose. And as a result of his decisions and the ensuing efforts he made to make those goals a reality, medical and electrical uses for atomic power were found.

He also gave speeches and helped stir up interest in a worldwide peacekeeping force that eventually culminated in the founding of the United Nations.

"Nothing contributes so much to tranquilizing the mind," wrote Mary Wollstonecraft Shelly, "as a steady purpose — a point on which the soul may fix its intellectual eye."

It is physically and psychologically healthy for a human being to have a strong sense of purpose — to feel motivated. The state of mind you have when you're absorbed in the accomplishment of a purpose is called "flow," which is a pleasantly engaged state of focus. Those who have learned to develop a sense of purpose and who have learned to become engrossed in the achievement of purposes are more likely to be happy and healthy. This has been shown in scientific studies and in everyday observations.

Happy people are *purposeful* people because the most reliable self-created source of happiness is taking action along a strongly-held purpose.

Flow has been the subject of quite a bit of research. For example, swimmers who experienced flow while training made the most progress by the end of the training. In other words, *experiencing frequent flow* allowed them to develop their abilities faster.

Another study accentuated those findings. It found that of all the things that influence how successful a person might become in their sport or skill — in *whatever* field — the most influential factor was how much flow they experienced while doing it. In other words, the amount of absorption they had was the *best* predictor of who would develop their talent the most.

A sense of purpose brings out the best in people. In his book, *Carrying the Fire: An Astronaut's Journeys*, Michael Collins wrote about the enthusiasm of the people in the Apollo space program in 1964. "…the goal was clearly and starkly defined," wrote Collins. "Had not President Kennedy said before the end of the decade?"

They had a clear goal that the people at NASA were excited about. The moon! The impossible goal! The goal they said could *never* be done! People showed up early, worked hard, and stayed late. They were intensely motivated.

As Collins put it, "People knew that each day was *one day closer* to putting man on the moon…" This is the electrifying power of a strong sense of purpose.

Mihaly Csikszentmihalyi, one of the principle researchers into flow, says we usually see work as a necessary evil, and we think *leisure* is what we want: time on our hands. Free time. Time with nothing to do. We *long* for it. And yet, he says, "free time is more difficult to enjoy than work."

Or as Jerome K. Jerome put it, "It is impossible to enjoy idling unless there is plenty of work to do."

Work provides clear goals more often than leisure and a clear goal is the first and most important requirement of flow.

If you want to experience flow, you must have a purpose. Work provides a purpose. It provides something to become absorbed in, so it provides opportunities for flow. To get flow from leisure, *you* have to provide the purpose. Many people don't know that, which means many people don't get much enjoyment from their coveted leisure; it isn't as satisfying as they wish it would be or expect it to be. Some even *suffer* during leisure.

Sandor Ferenczi, a psychoanalyst in the early 1900's discovered that anxiety and depression occurred more often on *Sundays* than any other day of the week. Since that time, many observers have noticed that vacations and retirement also tend to produce anxiety and depression.

When we are not on the job — when we are not given a clear purpose — many of us feel adrift and don't know what's missing. Clearly, a large percentage of people don't have a strong sense of purpose during their time off, and it's a shame. Purpose is king.

A purpose to sink your teeth into gives your mind a healthy, productive focus and prevents it from drifting into negativity. Without goals, wrote Csikszentmihalyi, "the mind begins to wander, and more often than not it will focus on unresolvable problems that cause anxiety."

POWER OF CAUSE

In addition to their function in producing flow, goals put you in a *causal* position (as opposed to a victim position) and that is good for your psychological well-being.

Purpose has an almost magical quality. It can imbue us with extraordinary ability. It can make us almost superhuman — more capable than humans in an ordinary state.

Ulysses S. Grant was writing his autobiography near the end of his life. His publisher was Mark Twain. Even though Grant was famous and had been President, he was broke. He had essentially been swindled out of his money.

Twain had assured Grant there was a market for his memoirs if he could finish it. But Grant had throat cancer and was dying. But he *couldn't* die. He had something he needed to accomplish. It was very important to him to finish this book and do a good job because if he didn't, he would leave his wife destitute when he died. This was his last chance.

So he persisted. He experienced intense pain. He couldn't swallow without pain. It was increasingly difficult to eat. When he could no longer write, he dictated. Doctors said he might not live more than two or three weeks, but like I said, purpose has a mysterious power, and Grant continued working on his book until he finished it.

He died five days after he completed his manuscript. And, by the way, Twain was right: The book, *Personal Memoirs of Ulysses S. Grant*, was very successful and is even to this day considered one of the best military memoirs ever written. Grant's wife, Julia, was set for life. He achieved his goal, fought his last heroic campaign, and stayed alive long enough to do it.

Charles Schulz declared many months ahead of time when he was going to end his comic strip. His last strip was published Sunday. The night before, Schulz died in his sleep.

After his family was shipwrecked, Dougal Robertson started adding up their stock. He discovered they had enough food and water to last ten days. They were two hundred miles downwind and downcurrent from the Galapagos Islands — it would be an impossible feat to sail there with their dingy. They were 2800 miles from the Marquesas Islands, but without a compass or means of finding their position, their chance of missing the islands was enormous. The Central American coast was a thousand miles away, but they had to make it through the windless Doldrums. They wouldn't be missed by anyone for five weeks, and nobody would have the slightest idea of where to start looking anyway, so waiting for rescue would have been suicide.

There were two possible places to be rescued by shipping vessels. One four hundred miles south; the other three hundred miles north.

Having roused himself enough to assess his situation accurately, his heart sank again. Their true and accurate situation wasn't very hopeful. His wife, Lyn, saw the look on his face and put her hand on his. She said simply, "We must get these boys to land."

This singular, clear purpose focused his mind through the entire journey. It galvanized his resolve. The thought kept coming back to him, spurring him on, making him try even when it seemed hopeless. This is the power of a definite, heartfelt purpose.

They all made it to shore alive. He got those boys to land.

THE MEANING OF LIFE

Purpose gives meaning to your life. In many ways, your purpose *is* the meaning of your life. That gives this subject a superimposing importance.

Viktor Frankl was a Jewish psychiatrist in Germany when Hitler took power, and he spent many years struggling to stay alive in concentration camps. During that time, he lost his wife, his brother, and both his parents — they either died in the camps or were sent to the gas chambers. He lost every possession he ever owned.

Because he already knew a lot about psychology and then experienced these extreme circumstances — and even managed to find meaning in his struggle — his slim book, *Man's Search for Meaning*, is powerful reading. His perspective on finding meaning in life is different from any other I have encountered. He writes:

> The meaning of life differs from person to person, from day to day and from hour to hour. What matters, therefore, is not the meaning of life in general but rather the specific meaning of a person's life at a given moment. To put the question in general terms would be comparable to the question posed to a chess champion, "Tell

me, Master, what is the best move in the world?" There simply is no such thing as the best or even a good move apart from a particular situation in a game and the particular personality of one's opponent. The same holds true for human existence. One should not search for an abstract meaning of life. Everyone has his own specific vocation or mission in life to carry out a concrete assignment which demands fulfillment.

I love that line: "…to carry out a concrete assignment which demands fulfillment." And Frankl provides many good examples of what he means. For example, he tried to keep his fellow prisoners from committing suicide. But the Nazi camps strictly *forbade* prisoners from stopping someone who was killing himself. If you cut down a fellow prisoner in the process of hanging himself, you (and probably everyone in your bunkhouse) would be severely punished.

So Frankl had to catch people *before they actually attempted* to kill themselves. This, he felt, was a concrete assignment which demanded fulfillment. He was a psychiatrist and he was the most qualified to answer this call from life.

The men would often confide in Frankl, since he was a psychiatrist. At two different times, two men told him they had decided to commit suicide. Both of them offered the same reason: They had nothing more to expect from life. All they could expect was endless suffering, starvation, torture, and in the end, probably the gas chamber.

"In both cases," wrote Frankl, "it was a question of getting them to realize that *life* was still expecting something from them; something in the future was expected of *them*."

After talking with the men, he found one of them was a scientist who had written several volumes of a book, but the project was incomplete. It couldn't be finished by anyone else. The other man had a child in another country waiting for him.

Each of our lives is unique. The concrete assignment needing to be fulfilled is different for every person. And Frankl found that a person would not commit suicide once they realized their specific obligation to life — in Frankl's words, that life expected something of them.

Michael W. Fox, a veterinarian and author of *Superdog: Raising the Perfect Canine Companion*, was a lover of animals from a very young age, as many kids are. One day he was walking home from school when he looked through a fence and saw a ghastly sight. It was the backyard of a veterinary clinic, and there was a large trash bin overflowing with dead dogs and cats.

"I never knew the reason for this mass extermination," Fox said, "but I was, from that time on, committed to doing all I could to help animals, deciding at age nine that I had to be a veterinarian."

Here was *a concrete assignment* life had presented to Fox, and he answered the call. He became a veterinarian and has done what he could to reduce the suffering of animals. He has spent his life educating people, writing books, and lobbying to create new legislation that reflects more respect for animals.

Dr. Seuss had a mission when he started. He wanted to get children interested in reading. "Before Seuss," wrote Peter Bernstein, "too many children's writers seemed locked into plots that ended with a heavy-handed call to obey one's elders. By the 1950s, educators were warning that America was losing a whole generation of readers."

Dr. Seuss wanted to do something about that. It felt to him like a concrete assignment that demanded fulfillment. And he fulfilled it. He wrote books kids *wanted* to read. The *Cat in the Hat, Green Eggs and Ham, How the Grinch Stole Christmas, And to Think That I Saw It on Mulberry Street, Horton Hears a Who!* and forty-three others which have sold over *two hundred million* copies worldwide.

And he awakened an entire *generation* to a love of reading.

The best goal is something heartfelt. Psychologist Allen Wiesen wrote, "The need for meaning in life goes far beyond the mechanical techniques of selecting a goal to be achieved by positive thinking. If a person selects a goal just to satisfy the demands of others he will quickly revert back to self-defeating trap circuits. He will rapidly lose ambition, and though he may try to appear as if he is succeeding in what he is doing, he will feel miserable because he is not really committed to this objective. All the success seminars in the world will not make a potential Mozart or Monet content to be president of the Chase Manhattan Bank."

YOU MUST HAVE A GOAL

During the Korean War, the Chinese government systematically tried to brainwash the U.S. POWs. Their methods included deprivation and torture, and the captives suffered tremendously. At one point, in one of the prison camps, three-fourths of the POWs had died. Things were incredibly bleak for the rest of them, and they were all feeling desperate and hopeless.

Then one man said to the others, "We've got to stay alive, we've got to let others know about the horrors of Communism. We've got to live to bring back the armies and fight these evil people. Communism must not win!"

This was a turning point for every man there because their meaningless struggle was transformed into a mission. Simply staying alive against the odds was their goal. Their despair was turned into resolve. Their hopelessness turned into determination. And their death rate went way down.

Speaking again of his experience in a concentration camp, Frankl wrote, "As we said before, any attempt to restore a man's inner strength in the camp had first to succeed in showing him some future goal...Woe to him who saw no more sense in his life, no aim, no purpose, and therefore no point in carrying on. He was soon lost."

Sometimes it takes a scientific study to prove the obvious. At least you find out that what you think is self-evident is actually true. Researchers at New York State Psychiatric Institute asked an unusual question of suicidal people. Rather than asking what makes them want to *die*, the researchers asked what makes them want to *live*.

They studied eighty-four people who were suffering with major depression and tried to figure out why thirty-nine of them had *never* attempted to kill themselves.

The study revealed that age, sex, religious persuasion, education level — none of these predicted who would attempt suicide. But *not having a reason to live* predicted it rather well. The depressed patients who perceived life as more worth living were less likely to attempt to kill themselves. People with a reason to live were less likely to kill themselves. Duh.

So now we know: Goals are very important. It is not just a nice thing. It's *vital*. Get yourself *a concrete assignment that demands fulfillment*. Look for something that fires you up, that you think is *needed*, that you feel is *important*, and that you can do something about.

If someone has no purpose at all, a small goal is a big improvement. But as the level of mental health increases, there comes a time when a full-on *mission* is called for as a context for your life.

You can still watch movies. You can still spend time connecting with your loved ones. Walk in the woods. Go on vacation. But like a mantra you constantly return to, your definite purpose, your concrete assignment, is always there to give you a sense of purpose and meaning to your existence. And, of course, a strong and steady motivation.

RIGHT NOW

Even if you have a large, overarching purpose, you can only take action in this very moment. It is an excellent practice to try to keep in mind one clear purpose for what you're doing now. And the question, "What is my purpose here?" can really straighten up and clarify your mind and your actions.

For example, if you are criticizing someone, ask yourself, "What am I after?" You may find what you're really after is to make the other person feel bad or punish them for something they did. That is the *automatic*, genetically-driven (and usually counterproductive) purpose. In other words, you didn't really consciously *choose* to pursue that goal. It happened without you. But now that you've asked the question, "What is my purpose here?" you can choose. You can think about what you really want in this situation.

You may decide you really want the person not to do it again. Then you'd have a clear purpose and a clear path for action — a path without games or negative feelings.

Make it a regular practice to ask yourself what you want right now. What is your goal here in this situation? Always and *consciously* be clear about what your purpose is in this very moment. It is effective. It is therapeutic. It is healthy. And it will make you more productive.

One key to a strong sense of purpose and motivation is the practice of focusing *only* on what you *want*. When your mind wanders to other things, *bring your focus back*. Again and again. Your mind is very easily taken off track, so you have to keep noticing your attention has wandered and keep bringing your focus back to your purpose. This is how to stay on track. This is what *specifically* you can do to stay focused.

When your mind starts worrying about problems that might happen, bring your mind back to your concrete assignment. When your attention becomes fixed on what you *don't* want, turn your attention to what you *do* want.

Keep your attention on the goal, and your sense of purpose will grow strong.

There isn't one "right" purpose which you must find and follow. Delete that kind of magical thinking from your thoughts forever! Any (constructive) purpose *is better than no purpose* and some are better than others. Some are good for now, but no good if pursued too long. The important thing is that you *like* the purpose and feel motivated about it.

SETTING YOUR COURSE

If you don't already have a strong purpose, how do you go about creating one? A high-quality purpose is more than something you feel you *should* do. That isn't good enough. A good purpose is something you feel a strong desire to do, even feel *compelled* to do, and something you feel is important — something you think *needs* to be done and ought to be done because it is right and good. Or something you feel strongly *interested* in, something that fascinates you and fills you with interest and curiosity.

If nothing comes to mind right now, that's not the end of the conversation. There is no such legitimate answer as, "I don't have one of those." Yes, you do. You may have forgotten it. You may never have dug deeply enough to find it in the first place. But you've got at least one. And all you need is one.

Most likely there was a time when you knew what your purpose was, at least in a general sense, but for one reason or another you discarded it; maybe someone convinced you it was impossible or stupid, or you maybe convinced yourself. It's now as if you've turned your back on it and are looking around saying, "I don't see any purpose I really want." No, of course not. It is behind you, so to speak. You've already picked it up, had it in your hand and then tossed it behind you where you are no longer looking.

Start right now with the assumption that there is a purpose which strongly compels you or strongly interests you, and commit yourself to finding it.

If you didn't already have a purpose, now you have one: Finding it. What interests you? What do you like to talk about? What do you daydream about? What do you think needs to be done? What do you think "someone" ought to do? What do you "wish you could do" but know you can't?

A high quality purpose is concrete, challenging, and something you feel is achievable. That's where flow is. That's where motivation is. That's where confidence is. That's where ability is formed. *That's where the fun is.*

In a study at the University of Alabama, they found that people who considered their goal difficult but achievable were more motivated — they were more energized and felt their goal was more important than someone who had either an easy goal or an impossible goal.

People who thought their goal was *easy* weren't as motivated. And people who thought their goal was *impossible* weren't motivated either. Remember, *difficult but achievable*. Not achievable in some abstract sense, but something *you* feel *you* could achieve. And something you feel challenged by.

John French, Jr., director of the project, did a study of 2,010 men in twenty-three different jobs, trying to find out which jobs were the most stressful. What they found was kind of surprising. The most stressful jobs were the most boring and unchallenging. These were the jobs that produced the most physical and emotional illness.

Says French, "One of the key factors in job satisfaction is self-utilization — the opportunity to fully utilize your abilities on the job, to be challenged, to develop yourself. Frustration and anxiety over not being challenged can have physically debilitating effects."

A big, challenging goal, if you feel up to it, will awaken the genius within, bring out your latent talents, give you satisfaction, and make the world a better place. Beethoven's goal was to create music that would transcend fate. Socrates had a goal to make people happy by making them reasonable and just. These are big goals, but they brought out the best in these people and wrote their names in history.

THE PURPOSE KILLER

Probably the biggest killer of purpose is all-or-nothing thinking. "I want to sail around the world," says a young man. But he is married and has a new baby. Obviously he can't go sailing around the world. Or can he? If he's thinking in all-or-nothing terms, he will, of course say, "No, I can't go sailing around the world unless I want to be a jerk and leave my wife and child." But that's thinking in terms of one extreme or the other, and life very rarely needs to be so black-or-white.

He wakes up one night with a realization. He has been blinding himself with all-or-nothing thinking! He comes up with a plan. He begins to set aside twenty dollars a week in a Sailing Fund.

As he does better at work, he increases that weekly amount. For now, he uses the money for sailing lessons and boating safety classes and books on celestial navigation, always leaving aside a little to accumulate for the purchase of an actual boat. He learns about boat design.

It takes him a little less than three years before he learns enough to decide what design of boat he wants to get. It takes him another year to figure out what course he will chart, what places he will visit, etc. As his son gets older, they go sailing together on rented sailboats. His son learns how to sail. The father teaches him how to reef the sails, how to steer, how to navigate by the stars.

All along the way, his purpose *is giving him life.* By the time his son is fourteen, the family decides to go for it. They sell their house, buy a sailboat, fill it with supplies, and what do you know? His purpose wasn't silly or impossible after all. It may be, in fact, the highlight of his family's life.

Another thing that kills dreams or prevents the development of a strong sense of purpose is that your interest might die. But here you have to be careful. Did your interest die because you actually lost interest now that you know more about it, or did your interest die because of demoralization — because of the way you're explaining setbacks to yourself?

There are certain ways to explain setbacks in your life that will kill your enthusiasm, destroy your interest, and prevent the development of a sense of purpose.

If your interest has been killed by a feeling of defeat, you can revive that dormant interest and fill your life with purpose and meaning.

It's important that the goals you seek give you a sense of meaning — that they aren't only about material gain. It's true that any goal is better than no goal, but it's also true that if you have a choice, you ought to choose high-quality goals, goals that will give you a great deal of satisfaction and even meaning.

Susan Krause Whitbourne conducted a long-term research project, starting in 1966. In that time, she saw a particular psychological measurement steadily decline over the years. It's called "ego integrity," which is a composite characteristic having to do with honesty, a sense of connection with others, a sense of wholeness, and a feeling that life has meaning.

Between 1977 and 1988, ego integrity took a universal dive. The life-satisfaction scores were *as low as they could go* on her measurements. "People got caught up in chasing the materialistic dream," says Whitbourne, "They got recognition for their achievements, yet don't feel that what they are doing matters in the larger scheme of things."

SIMPLIFICATION OF PURPOSES

John is a waiter, and he discovered a fundamental principle of life. When he only has one table, he isn't stressed at all. He can concentrate and do a good job, and it is no problem. Two tables, okay. Still no problem. Three tables, and he has to start really paying attention, because it's like juggling — the more balls you have in the air, the easier it is to drop one. When John gets up to seven or eight tables, it becomes *stressful.* The juggling of tasks becomes too complex to handle well.

In the same way, the number of purposes you have is directly related to your stress hormone level. Depending on how you handle your goals, a strong sense of purpose and motivation can help you manage stress well, or it can make your general stress level much worse.

The problem is that the natural drift for people is toward *complication.* In other words, if you don't try to do anything about it, your life will get more and more complicated; you will collect more and more purposes.

As you've learned, you have to make a continuous effort to simplify your purposes. Your life will naturally and constantly drift toward complication, just as a rose bush will constantly try to sprawl. You must *continually* prune. You can't prune once and for all. You have to *keep* pruning.

For example, John wanted his guests to be happy. That was one of his purposes. He also wanted to get along well with his fellow waiters. And he wanted to please the cooks so their interactions were pleasant. And, of course, he wanted his managers to be happy with him. And so on. He has too many purposes. His attention is scattered in too many directions. If he knew about simplifying purposes, he would trim his purposes down to something *manageable*. For example, to make his guests pleased with his service. That's enough to concentrate on, and that would keep his tension level lower, because it is manageable.

Manage your purposes. Make a list. What are the really important purposes? Trim the list down to something manageable; *something simple enough* that you can manage it without stress.

Get few enough purposes that it *feels good*.

Be aware that after you trim your purposes, complexity will gradually creep back in. Simplifying your purposes is something you'll need to do once in awhile for the rest of your life.

Keep your purposes strong and clear, simple and heartfelt, and you will find the most powerful source of self-generated happiness that exists in this world: The fire within.

"This is the true joy in life, the being used for a purpose recognized by yourself as a mighty one; the being thoroughly worn out before you are thrown on the scrap heap; the being a force of Nature instead of a feverish selfish little clod of ailments and grievances complaining that the world will not devote itself to making you happy."

- George Bernard Shaw

About the Author

Adam Khan blogs at adamlikhan.com, hosts the The Adam Bomb podcast, and he is the author of the books, *Self-Help Stuff That Works*, *Principles For Personal Growth* (now being used as a textbook for a college course in San Diego), *What Difference Does It Make: How the Sexes Differ and What You Can Do About It*, *How to Change the Way You Look at Things (in Plain English)*, *Antivirus For Your Mind*, *Slotralogy*, and *Self-Reliance, Translated*.

Adam has been published in *Prevention Magazine*, *Cosmopolitan*, *Body Bulletin*, *Your Personal Best Newsletter*, *Wisdom*, *Think and Grow Rich Newsletter*, *the Success Strategies* newsletter, and he was a regular columnist for *At Your Best* (a Rodale Press publication) for seven years where his monthly column was voted the readers' favorite. You can write to him at adamkhan@usa.com.